MW01031861

THE LONG DARKNESS

Contributors

Henry Steele Commager is Simpson Lecturer at Amherst College. His books include *The American Mind; An Interpretation of American Thought and Character since the 1880s*.

Erik H. Erikson is Professor of Human Development, Emeritus, Harvard University.

Jerome D. Frank is Professor Emeritus of Psychiatry at the Johns Hopkins University School of Medicine. His major professional field is psychotherapy, in which he has published extensively. For some thirty years he has been engaged in seeking to apply psychological insights to the resolution of the nuclear armaments predicament. He is active in several antinuclear organizations and has contributed many articles to professional journals on this subject as well as a book *Sanity and Survival in the Nuclear Age* (Random House, 1982).

Stephen Jay Gould is Professor of Geology and Alexander Agassiz Professor of Biology, Harvard University.

Lester Grinspoon is Associate Professor of Psychiatry, Harvard Medical School.

J. Bryan Hehir is the Secretary for Social Affairs at the U.S. Catholic Bishops Conference in Washington, D.C., a Senior Research Scholar at the Kennedy Institute of Ethics and Research Professor of Ethics and International Politics at Georgetown University.

Robert Jay Lifton is Distinguished Professor of Psychiatry and Psychology, The City University of New York, at John Jay College of Criminal Justice, and The Graduate School and University Center, The Mount Sinai School of Medicine. His books include *Death in Life: Survivors of Hiroshima; The Broken Connection: On Death and the Continuity of Life;* and most recently (with Richard Falk), *Indefensible Weapons: The Political and Psychological Case against Nuclearism;* and (with Nicholas Humphrey) *In a Dark Time*.

John E. Mack is Professor and Chairman of the Executive Committee, Harvard Department of Psychiatry. He was awarded the Pulitzer Prize in biography in 1977 for *A Prince of Our Disorder: The Life of T. E. Lawrence.* He has for several years been studying some of the psychological and psychiatric dimensions of the nuclear arms race.

Carl Sagan is David Duncan Professor of Astronomy and Space Sciences and Director of the Laboratory for Planetary Studies at Cornell University. He has played a leading role in the exploration of the solar system by robot spacecraft. He is a recipient of the Pulitzer Prize and, with his colleagues, was recently awarded the Leo Szilard Award for Physics in the Public Interest of the American Physical Society for the discovery of nuclear winter.

The LONG

DARKNESS

PSYCHOLOGICAL AND
MORAL PERSPECTIVES
ON NUCLEAR WINTER

EDITED BY Lester Grinspoon

Yale University Press
NEW HAVEN AND LONDON

This book grew out of a symposium that was presented in Los Angeles as part of the scientific Program of the 1983 Annual Meeting of the American Psychiatric Association. The views expressed by the contributors do not necessarily represent the American Psychiatric Association.

Copyright © 1986 by Yale University.
All rights reserved.
This book may not be reproduced, in whole or in part, in any form (beyond that copying permitted by Sections 107 and 108 of the U.S. Copyright Law and except by reviewers for the public press), without written permission from the publishers.

Designed by Susan P. Fillion.
Set in Baskerville text and Helvetica display type and printed in the United States of America by Vail-Ballou Press, Binghamton, N.Y.

The paper in this book meets the guidelines for permanence and durability of the Committee on Production Guidelines for Book Longevity of the Council on Library Resources.

Library of Congress Cataloging-in-Publication Data
Main entry under title:

The Long darkness: psychological and moral perspectives on nuclear winter.

Grew out of a symposium in Los Angeles of the Scientific Program of the 1983 annual meeting of the American Psychiatric Association.
    Bibliography: p.
    Includes index.
    1. Nuclear warfare—Psychological aspects—Congresses. 2. Nuclear warfare—Moral and ethical aspects—Congresses. 3. Nuclear winter—Congresses. I. Grinspoon, Lester, 1928–   . II. American Psychiatric Association. Meeting.
U263.L664 1986   355'.0217   84-40986
ISBN 0-300-03663-9 (alk. paper)
ISBN 0-300-03664-7 (pbk. : alk, paper)

10 9 8 7 6 5 4 3 2

Contents

vii

To the
Women and Men
of
Physicians for Social Responsibility

Introduction

LESTER GRINSPOON

The crisis we are asking the reader to consider is the most important one that has ever faced humanity and the hardest to examine seriously and steadily. Everyone who truly addresses it accepts the burden of disturbed serenity and complacency. Many people recognize in some way and at some level that the continuation of the nuclear arms race is a threat to the survival of civilization, nothing less—maybe even, as Dr. Sagan will demonstrate, to the survival of the human species. It is easy to repeat such words, and they have been spoken so often that we no longer hear them; the difficult thing is to make ourselves feel what we know and determine our actions by it. For once this knowledge is truly assimilated, once we have grasped it affectively as well as cognitively, it demands that we redirect our lives in small and large ways. It changes attitudes toward professional life, friendships, marriage, and especially children, including those as yet unborn. It also forces us to become more sensitive to the increasing extent to which our young children and adolescents perceive the threat of nuclear extermination as part of their lives and how these young people who see themselves as having an endangered future retreat into the present. And we cannot ignore the possible consequences of this retreat for their development.

It is natural and even healthy to want to get on with the business of our lives rather than think about a peril to all life that most of us prefer to see as abstract and remote. We do not want to be overwhelmed by anxiety, so we tend to keep the facts we know separate from our feelings.

The late Archibald MacLeish wrote, "Knowledge without feelings is not knowledge, and can only lead to public irresponsibility and indifference, conceivably to ruin. . . . [When] the fact is dissociated from the feel of the fact . . . that people, that civilization is in danger" (*Atlantic Monthly* 203 [1959]:40–46). Many people repress their fear, anger, and rebelliousness in response to the nuclear threat; instead they anesthetize themselves. They avoid acquiring information that would make vague fears specific enough to require decisive action; they contrive to ignore the implications of the information they do allow to get through; they resign their responsibilities to leaders and experts; they treat the accelerating nuclear arms race as simply none of their business and convince themselves that there is nothing they can do about it. Just as some dangers are too slight to arouse concern, this one is, paradoxically, too vast to arouse concern.

It is not an easy task to help people grasp affectively as well as cognitively the immensity of the danger. This is not just because we are all so psychologically well equipped to defend ourselves against anxiety that might threaten to overwhelm, but also because the horror itself is so abstract. Physicians, even though their work is often pressured and stressful, continue to be the professional group that smokes the least, and among physicians, thoracic surgeons have the lowest prevalence of smoking. Clearly, direct exposure to the consequences of smoking makes it difficult to deny them. Similarly, physicians have been in the vanguard of the movement to arouse the consciousness of the populace to the dangers of nuclear war. Working in the emergency room makes suffering from blast, fire, cold, radiation sickness, starvation, and infectious disease less of an abstraction. People who have or have had such experience are less likely to suffer from this failure of imagination.

We have to confront the truth in this unprecedented situation. We must rouse ourselves from complacency and passivity and assume responsibility. We need the courage to be afraid and to make our friends, neighbors, and colleagues afraid—with a fear that is not neurotic and panicky but thoughtful, a fear not so much for ourselves as for our children, for civilization, and for this precious world.

A problem for anyone who fully assimilates a consciousness of the nuclear threat is that it requires us to redirect our thoughts and change our lives in certain ways—a demand that many people understandably prefer to avoid. It means taking some time that we would like to devote to interesting, self-fulfilling work with obvious rewards and devoting it instead to what seems a frustrating, unfulfilling struggle with few intrinsic rewards and an uncertain chance of success. It does not even bring the pleasure of correcting a visible injustice or relieving visible suffering. In fact, like some techniques of psychotherapy, it heightens suffering in the short run for everyone who is shaken out of numbness or self-delusion and into confrontation of the reality.

Psychiatrists have an important role in developing more understanding of how to make these truths available to everyone. Psychotherapy itself is a model for the process of allowing people to deal constructively with disturbing truths. And as psychiatrists we should be strongly impelled to help others confront this unparalleled threat, because our experience makes us acutely aware of both aspects of the situation: the human potential for irrational and self-destructive acts, and also the enormous human capacity for altruism, adaptation, and creative solutions to the most difficult of problems.

We know now that the nuclear danger is even more terrible than we have supposed. The reader may recall that at one point in the Stanley Kubrick movie *Dr. Strangelove*, the title character asks the Soviet ambassador, "You mean you built a doomsday machine and you didn't tell anybody?" The question was meant to be ludicrous and the doomsday machine a fantasy, but in the December 23, 1983, issue of *Science*, Dr. Sagan and a group of fellow scientists reported an astonishing discovery: the superpowers have inadvertently built a doomsday machine, and it is operational at this very moment. As in the film, the governments of the superpowers are not telling anybody. They behave as though they do not believe it themselves, let alone feel any obligation to let the inhabitants of the planet know of this threat to their survival. Until great numbers of people come to genuinely appreciate the magnitude of this danger to themselves and future generations and demand of their governments that they reverse the arms race, the risk of setting off the doomsday machine will increase.

The Austrian poet and satirist Karl Kraus wrote in 1917, during the darkest days of World War I, "If we still had imagination, we would no longer wage war." If the people of Europe had been able to conceive the horrors of trench warfare, they would not have acquiesced in the policies that made it inevitable. Nuclear war is infinitely more horrible and more difficult to imagine, and most people, including many in high office, do not attempt to imagine it. The authors of this book are contributing to a struggle against unimaginativeness and insensibility either imposed by circumstances or deliberately cultivated. Dr. Sagan will describe the consequences of a nuclear war; the other authors will explain how we have become trapped into risking these consequences and how political use of the nuclear threat affects our lives.

H. G. Wells once pointed out that human history has become more and more a race between education and catastrophe; the race has become even more desperate since then. A terrible thought is that our education might be provided by catastrophe itself, by nuclear destruction short of nuclear war—a nuclear weapon detonated by mechanical error or human error or madness—an accident more devastating by orders of magnitude than the one at Three Mile Island that helped so much to educate us about industrial nuclear power. That would be learning the hardest way of all. We present this book in the hope that a better kind of education is still possible, that if we allow ourselves to learn and think about what is being prepared for us, and in our name, we will reject it and make it our business to work for a change.

Nuclear War and Climatic Catastrophe: Some Policy Implications

CARL SAGAN

It is not even impossible to imagine that the effects of an atomic war fought with greatly perfected weapons and pushed by the utmost determination will endanger the survival of man.

EDWARD TELLER
Bulletin of the Atomic Scientists 3, 35 (February 1947).

The extreme danger to mankind inherent in the proposal [by Edward Teller and others to develop thermonuclear weapons] wholly outweighs any military advantage.

J. ROBERT OPPENHEIMER ET AL.
Report of the General Advisory Committee,
U.S. Atomic Energy Commission, October 1949.

The fact that no limits exist to the destructiveness of this weapon makes its very existence and the knowledge of its construction a danger to humanity. . . . It is . . . an evil thing.

ENRICO FERMI & I. I. RABI
Addendum, ibid.

A very large nuclear war would be a calamity of indescribable proportions and absolutely unpredictable consequences, with the uncertainties tending toward the worst. . . . All-out nuclear war would mean the destruction of contemporary civilization, throw man back centuries, cause the death of hundreds of millions or billions of people, and, with a certain degree of probability, would cause man to be destroyed as a biological species.

ANDREI SAKHAROV
Foreign Affairs, 61, 1001 (1983).

To be taken seriously, apocalyptic predictions require higher standards of evidence than do assertions on other matters where the stakes are not as great. Since the immediate effects of even a single thermonuclear weapon explosion are so devastating, it is natural to assume—even without considering detailed mechanisms—that the more or less simultaneous explosion of ten thousand such weapons all over the Northern Hemisphere might have unpredictable and catastrophic consequences.

And yet, while it is widely accepted that a full nuclear war might mean the end of civilization, at least in the Northern Hemisphere, claims that nuclear war might imply a reversion of the human population to prehistoric levels, or even the extinction of the human species, have, among some policymakers at least, been dismissed as alarmist or, worse, irrelevant. Popular works that stress this theme, such as Nevil Shute's *On the Beach* and Jonathan Schell's *The Fate of the Earth,* have been labeled disreputable. The apocalyptic claims are rejected as unproved and unlikely, and it is judged unwise to frighten the public with doomsday talk when nuclear weapons are needed, we are told, to preserve the peace. But, as the epigraphs that open this chapter illustrate, comparably dire warnings have been made by respectable scientists with diverse political inclinations, including many of the American and Soviet physicists who conceived, devised, and constructed the world nuclear arsenals.[1]

A somewhat briefer version of this chapter appeared in *Foreign Affairs* 62, no. 2 (Winter 1983–84): 257–292.
    1. And many others. The following impression of early thermonuclear weapons explosions by Thomas E. Murray in 1953, then commissioner of the U.S. Atomic Energy Commission, is typical: "Had you been with me last fall, out in the Pacific at our testing station at Eniwetok, you would have no doubt that mankind now has within the range of his grasp means to exterminate the human race."

Part of the resistance to serious consideration of such apocalyptic pronouncements is their necessarily theoretical basis. Understanding the long-term consequences of nuclear war is not a problem amenable to experimental verification—at least not more than once. Another part of the resistance is psychological. Most people—recognizing nuclear war as a grave and terrifying prospect and nuclear policy as immersed in technical complexities, official secrecy, and bureaucratic inertia—tend to practice what psychiatrists call denial: putting the agonizing problem out of our heads, since there seems nothing we can do about it. Even policymakers must feel this temptation from time to time. But for policymakers there is another concern: if it turns out that nuclear war could end our civilization or our species, such a finding might be considered a retroactive rebuke to those responsible, actively or passively, in the past or in the present, for the global nuclear arms race.

The stakes are too high for us to permit any such factors to influence our assessment of the consequences of nuclear war. If nuclear war now seems significantly more catastrophic than has generally been believed in the military and policy communities, then serious consideration of the resulting implications is urgently called for. It is in that spirit that this chapter attempts, first, to present a short summary, in lay terms, of the climatic and biological consequences of nuclear war that emerge from extensive scientific studies conducted over the past two years, the essential conclusions of which have now been endorsed by a large number of scientists. These findings were presented in detail at a special conference in Cambridge, Massachusetts, involving almost one hundred scientists on April 22–26, 1983, and were publicly announced at a conference in Washington, D.C., on October 31 and November 1, 1983. A detailed statement of the findings and the underlying evidence has been published (Turco et al., TTAPS, 1983), as have a number of subsequent corroboratory studies (for summaries, see Covey et al., 1984; Chagas et al., 1984; National Research Council, 1985; Hare et al., 1985; Pittock et al., in press; Sagan, 1985). The present summary is designed particularly for the lay reader. Following this summary, I explore the possible strategic and policy implications of the new findings. They point to one apparently inescapable conclusion: the necessity of moving as rapidly as possible to reduce the global nuclear arsenals below levels that could conceivably cause the kind of climatic catastrophe and cascading biological devastation predicted by the new studies. Such a reduction would have to be to a small percentage of the present global strategic arsenals.

The Climatic Catastrophe

The immediate consequences of a single thermonuclear weapon explosion are well known and well documented (Glasstone & Dolan, 1977)—fireball radiation, prompt neutrons and gamma rays, blast, and fires. The Hiroshima bomb that killed between 100,000 and 200,000 people was a fission device of about 12 kilotons' yield (the explosive equivalent of 12,000 tons of TNT). A modern thermonuclear warhead uses a device something like the Hiroshima bomb as the trigger—the match to light the fusion reaction. A typical thermonuclear weapon might have a yield of about 500 kilotons (or 0.5 megatons, a megaton being the explosive equivalent of a million tons of TNT). There are many weapons in the 9- to 20-megaton range in the strategic arsenals of the United States (U.S.) and the Soviet Union (S.U.) today. The highest yield weapon ever exploded (set off by the S.U. in Novaya Zemlya on October 30, 1961) was 58 megatons.

Strategic nuclear weapons are those designed for delivery by ground-based or submarine-launched missiles, or by bombers, to targets in the adversary's homeland. Many weapons with yields roughly equal to that of the Hiroshima bomb are today assigned to "tactical" or "theater" military missions, or are designated "munitions" and relegated to ground-to-air and air-to-air missiles, torpedoes, depth charges, and artillery. While strategic weapons often have higher yields than tactical weapons, this is not always the case.[2] Modern tactical or theater missiles (for example, Pershing 2, SS-20) and air support (for example, F-15, MiG-23) have sufficient range to make the distinction between "strategic" and "tactical" or "theater" weapons increasingly artificial. Both categories of weapons can be delivered by land-based missiles, sea-based missiles, and aircraft, and by intermediate-range as well as intercontinental delivery systems. Nevertheless, by the usual accounting, there are around 18,000 strategic thermonuclear weapons and the equivalent number of fission triggers in the American and Soviet strategic arsenals, with an aggregate yield of about 10,000 megatons. The total number of nuclear weapons (strategic plus theater and tactical) in the arsenals of the two nations is close to 50,000, with an aggregate yield near 15,000 megatons. For convenience, we here collapse the distinction between strategic and theater weapons and adopt, under the rubric "strategic," an aggregate yield of 13,000 megatons. The nuclear weapons of the rest of the world—mainly Britain, France, and China—amount to many hundreds of warheads and a few hundred megatons of additional aggregate yield.

No one knows, of course, how many warheads with what aggregate yield would be detonated in a nuclear war. Because of attacks on strategic aircraft and missiles, and because of technological failures, it is clear that less than the entire world arsenal would be detonated. On the other hand, it is generally accepted, even among most military planners, that a "small" nuclear war would be almost impossible to contain before it escalated to include much of the world arsenals (see, for example, Ball, 1981; Bracken & Shubik, 1982, p. 155). (Precipitating factors include command and control malfunctions, communications failures, the necessity for in-

2. The "tactical" Pershing 1, for example, is listed as carrying warheads with yields as high as 400 kilotons, while the "strategic" Poseidon C-3 is listed with a yield of only 40 kilotons ("World Armaments and Disarmament, SIPRI Yearbook 1982," Stockholm International Peace Research Institute [London: Taylor & Francis, 1982], and J. Record, "U.S. Nuclear Weapons in Europe" [Washington, D.C.: Brookings Institution, 1974]).

stantaneous decisions on the fates of millions, fear, panic, and other aspects of real nuclear war fought by real people.) For this reason alone, any serious attempt to examine the possible consequences of nuclear war must place major emphasis on large-scale exchanges in the 5,000-to 7,000-megaton range—between about a third and a half of the world strategic inventories—and many studies have done so. (National Academy of Sciences, 1975; Office of Technology Assessment, 1979; Peterson, 1982; Bergstrom et al., 1983; Turco et al., 1983). Many of the effects described below, however, can be triggered by much smaller wars.

The adversary's strategic airfields, missile silos, naval bases, submarines at sea, weapons manufacturing and storage locales, civilian and military command and control centers, attack assessment and early warning facilities, and the like are probable targets ("counterforce attack"). While it is often stated that cities are not targeted "per se,"[3] many of the above targets are proximate to or collocated with cities, especially in Europe. In addition, there is an industrial targeting category ("countervalue attack"). Modern nuclear doctrines require that "war-supporting" facilities be attacked. Many of these facilities are necessarily industrial in nature and engage a work force of considerable size. They are almost always situated near major transportation centers so that raw materials and finished products can be efficiently transported to other industrial sectors or to forces in the field. Thus, such facilities are, almost by definition, cities, or near or within cities. Other "war-supporting" targets may include the transportation systems themselves (roads, canals, rivers, railways, civilian airfields), petroleum refineries, storage sites and pipelines, hydroelectric and nuclear power plants, radio and television transmitters, and the like. A major countervalue exchange therefore might involve almost all large cities in the U.S. and the S.U., and possibly most of the large cities in the North-

3. For U.S. targeting doctrines. Soviet and Chinese doctrines do not seem to be generally available. British and French doctrines are said to target cities, perhaps exclusively (e.g., Arthur Macy Cox, "End the War Game," *New York Times*, November 8, 1983).

ern Hemisphere (see, for example, Peterson, 1982). There are fewer than 2,500 cities in the world with over 100,000 inhabitants, so the devastation of all such cities is well within the means of the world nuclear arsenals.

Recent estimates of the immediate deaths from blast, prompt radiation, and fires in a major exchange in which cities were targeted range from several hundred million (Peterson, 1982) to—most recently, in a World Health Organization study in which targets were assumed not to be restricted entirely to NATO and Warsaw Pact countries—1.1 billion people. (Bergstrom et al., 1983). Serious injuries requiring immediate medical attention (which would be largely unavailable) would be suffered by a comparably large number of people (Peterson, 1982), perhaps an additional 1.1 billion (Bergstrom et al., 1983). Thus it is possible that virtually half the human population of the planet would be killed or seriously injured by the direct effects of a nuclear war. Social disruption; the unavailability of electricity, fuel, transportation, food deliveries, communications, and other civil services; the absence of medical care; the decline in sanitation measures; and rampant disease and severe psychiatric disorders would doubtless claim collectively a significant number of further victims. But a range of additional effects—some unexpected, some inadequately treated in earlier studies, some uncovered only recently—makes the picture much more somber still.

Destruction of missile silos, command and control facilities, and other hardened sites requires—because of current limitations on missile accuracy—nuclear weapons of fairly high yield exploded as groundbursts or as low airbursts. High-yield groundbursts will vaporize, melt, and pulverize the surface at the target area and propel large quantities of condensates and fine dust into the upper troposphere and stratosphere. The particles are chiefly entrained in the rising fireball; some ride up the stem of the mushroom cloud. Most military targets, however, are not very hard. The destruction of cities can be accomplished, as was demonstrated at Hiroshima and Nagasaki, by lower-yield explosions less than a kilometer above the surface. Low-yield airbursts over cities or near forests will tend to produce massive fires, in some cases over areas of 100,000 square kilometers or more. City fires generate enormous quantities of black oily smoke that rise at least into the upper part of the lower atmosphere, or troposphere (figure 1a). If firestorms occur, the smoke column rises vigorously, like the draft in a fireplace, and may (the question is still unresolved) carry some of the soot into the lower part of the upper atmosphere, or stratosphere. The smoke from forest and grassland fires would initially be restricted to the lower troposphere.

The fission of the (generally plutonium) trigger in every thermonuclear weapon and the reactions in the (generally uranium-238) casing added as a fission yield "booster" produce a witch's brew of radioactive products, which are also entrained in the cloud. Each such product, or radioisotope, has a characteristic half-life (defined as the time to decay to half of its original level of radioactivity). Most of the radioisotopes have very short half-lives and decay in hours to days. Particles injected into the stratosphere, mainly by high-yield explosions, fall out very slowly—characteristically in about a year, by which time most of the fission products, even when concentrated, will have decayed to much safer levels. Particles injected into the troposphere by low-yield explosions and fires fall out more rapidly—by gravitational settling, rainout, convection, and other processes—before the radioactivity has decayed to moderately safe levels. Thus rapid fallout of tropospheric radioactive debris tends to produce larger doses of ionizing radiation than does the slower fallout of radioactive particles from the stratosphere.

Nuclear explosions of more than 1 megaton yield generate a radiant fireball that rises through the troposphere into the stratosphere. The fireballs from weapons with yields between 100 kilotons and 1 megaton will partially extend into the stratosphere. The high temperatures in the fireball chemically ignite some of the nitrogen in the air, producing oxides of nitrogen, which in turn chemically attack and destroy the gas ozone in the middle stratosphere. But ozone

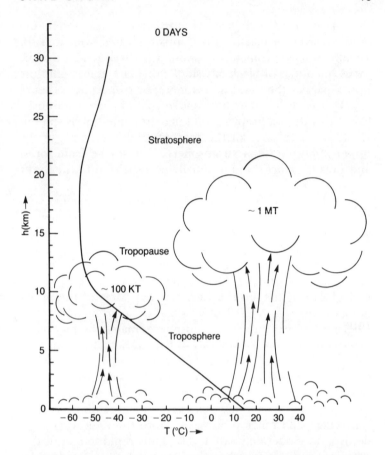

FIGURE 1a. An approximate representation of the ordinary temperature structure of the Earth's atmosphere at northern (or at southern) mid-latitudes. The surface, heated by the Sun, has an annual temperature of 13° C (56° F) on the average through the year. The temperature declines with altitude to a height of (h) about 13 kilometers (8 miles) where the temperature is −55° C (−67° F). These low temperatures are familiar to mountain climbers and airplane pilots. This lower region of the Earth's atmosphere, called the troposphere, is well mixed by winds and turbulence and experiences rainfall. Thus, fine particles will be carried out or rain out of the troposphere comparatively rapidly. The troposphere (and what we know as "weather") ends at the tropopause, at about 13 kilometers. Above it is the stratosphere. There, temperatures are more nearly constant with altitude,

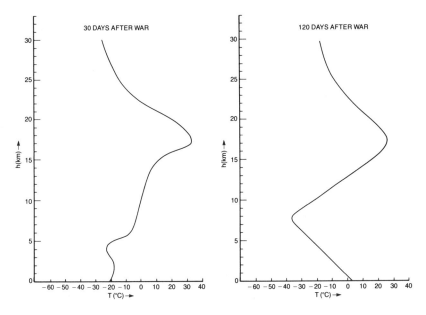

FIGURE 1b.   **FIGURE 1c.**

vertical winds and turbulence are mild, rainfall nonexistent, and fine particles fall out very slowly. Smoke from fires is mainly restricted to the troposphere, and the soot particles are removed comparatively rapidly. Dust from high-yield groundbursts—at silos and other hardened installations—is injected to a considerable extent into the stratosphere and falls out comparatively slowly. The explosive yield just barely able to inject material into the stratosphere is about 100 kilotons, as shown. The fireball from a 1-megaton explosion is almost entirely in the stratosphere. When the upper air is heated (through the absorption of sunlight by fine particles raised in the nuclear war), the surface is cooled because the same particles prevent sunlight from reaching the surface. In figure 1b, calculated from TTAPS results, the structure of the Earth's atmosphere at northern mid-latitudes 30 days after a baseline nuclear war is shown (case 1, table 1). As in figure 1a, the vertical axis represents height (h) and the horizontal axis indicates air temperature in degrees C. In figure 1c, the new temperature structure is shown after 120 days. In both cases the familiar atmospheric structure (figure 1a) has vanished, and a new temperature inversion region has appeared. This region is heated by the sunlight absorbed by the soot and dust. Just as for temperature inversions over cities such as Los Angeles, the altered temperature structure is very stable, and particles that have reached these altitudes are removed much more slowly than would ordinarily be the case. Since the in-

fluence of this temperature inversion is not yet included in the TTAPS calculations, the time scales for normal conditions to recover, shown in figure 2,
may be severe *under*estimates. In the 30-day case, the region in which the
temperature hardly varies wtih altitude has reached the ground, and in this
sense nuclear war can be said to bring the stratosphere down to Earth.

Comparison of these figures also helps explain why the fine particles tend
to stream, after a while, across the equator into the Southern Hemisphere.
Consider, e.g., an altitude of 10 kilometers in the Northern Hemisphere. A
few weeks after the baseline war, the temperatures there are around 0° C
(figure 1b). At the same altitude, in the as yet dust- and smoke-free Southern Hemisphere, the temperatures are 50° colder. Parcels of air, and the
particles they contain, will flow "downhill," from hotter regions to colder
ones. The large temperature contrasts will induce rising southward motion in
the Northern Hemisphere and sinking northward motion in the Southern
Hemisphere. The net effect may be to spread the dust-laden air globally and
to lift it even farther above the surface.

absorbs the biologically dangerous ultraviolet radiation from
the Sun. Thus the partial depletion of the stratospheric ozone
layer, or "ozonosphere," by high-yield nuclear explosions will
increase the flux of solar ultraviolet radiation at the surface
of the Earth (after the soot and dust have settled out). After
a nuclear war in which thousands of high-yield weapons are
detonated, the increase in biologically dangerous ultraviolet
light might be several hundred percent (Turco et al., 1983;
Ehrlich et al., 1983).[4] In the more dangerous shorter wave-
lengths, larger increases would occur. Nucleic acids and pro-
teins, the fundamental molecules for life on Earth, are especially sensitive to ultraviolet radiation. Thus, an increase
of the solar ultraviolet flux at the surface of the Earth is potentially dangerous for life.

These four effects—obscuring smoke in the troposphere,
obscuring dust in the stratosphere, the fallout of radioactive
debris, and the partial destruction of the ozone layer—con-
stitute the principal adverse environmental consequences that
we know would occur after a nuclear war is "over." There
may be others about which we are still ignorant. The dust
and, especially, the dark soot absorb ordinary visible light from

4. See also note 3.

the Sun, heating the atmosphere (figures 1b, 1c) and cooling the Earth's surface.

All four of these effects have been treated in our recent study, known from the initials of its authors as TTAPS. For the first time it is demonstrated that severe and prolonged low temperatures, the nuclear winter, would follow a nuclear war. (The study also explains the fact that no such climatic effects were detected after the detonation of hundreds of megatons during the period of U.S./S.U. atmospheric testing of nuclear weapons, ended by the limited test ban treaty in 1963: the explosions were sequential over many years, not virtually simultaneous; and, occurring over scrub desert, coral atolls, tundra, and wasteland, they set no fires.) The new results have been subjected to detailed scrutiny, and many corroboratory calculations have now been made, including at least two in the S.U. A special panel appointed by the National Academy of Sciences to examine this problem has come to similar conclusions.[5]

Unlike conclusions drawn in many previous studies, the effects do not seem to be restricted to northern mid-latitudes, where the nuclear exchange would mainly take place. There is now substantial evidence that the heating by sunlight of atmospheric dust and soot over northern mid-latitude targets would profoundly change the global circulation (see caption, figures 1b and 1c). Fine particles would be transported across the equator in weeks, bringing the cold and the dark to the Southern Hemisphere. (In addition, some studies—for example, Peterson, 1982—suggest that over 100 megatons would be dedicated to equatorial and Southern Hemisphere targets, thus generating fine particles locally.) Although it would be less cold and less dark at the ground in the Southern Hemisphere than in the Northern, massive climatic and environmental disruptions may be triggered there as well.

In our studies, several dozen different scenarios were chosen, covering a wide range of possible wars, and the range

5. See note 3.

of uncertainty in each key parameter was considered (for example, to describe how many fine particles are injected into the atmosphere). Five representative cases are shown in table 1, ranging from a small, low-yield attack exclusively on cities, utilizing only 0.8 percent of the world strategic arsenals, to a massive exchange involving 75 percent of the world strategic arsenals. "Nominal" cases assume the most probable parameter choices; "severe" cases assume adverse parameter choices, but still in the plausible range.

Predicted continental temperatures in the Northern Hemisphere vary after the nuclear war according to the curves shown in figure 2. The high heat capacity of water guarantees that oceanic temperatures will fall at most by a few degrees. Because temperatures are moderated by the adjacent oceans, temperatures in coastal regions will be less extreme than in continental interiors. The temperatures shown in figure 2 are average values for Northern Hemisphere land areas, with no account yet taken of the influence of the oceans or the initial patchiness of the clouds.

Even much smaller temperature declines are known to have serious consequences. The explosion of the Tambora volcano in Indonesia in 1815 led to an average global temperature decline of only 1° C, due to the obscuration of sunlight by the fine dust propelled into the stratosphere. The hard freezes the following year were so severe that 1816 has been known in Europe and America as "the year without a summer." A 1° C cooling would nearly eliminate wheat growing in Canada (National Academy of Sciences, 1975). Small global changes tend to be associated with considerably larger regional changes. In the past thousand years, the maximum global or Northern Hemisphere temperature deviations have been around 1° C. In an ice age, a typical long-term global temperature decline from preexisting conditions is about 10° C. Even the most modest of the cases illustrated in figure 2 give temporary temperature declines of this order. The baseline case is much more adverse. Unlike the situation in an ice age, however, the global temperatures after nuclear war would plunge rapidly and take only months to a few years

TABLE 1. Nuclear Exchange Scenarios

Case	Total Yield (MT)	% Yield Surface Bursts	% Yield Urban or Industrial Targets	Warhead Yield Range (MT)	Total Number of Explosions
1. Baseline case, countervalue and counterforce[a]	5,000	57	20	0.1–10	10,400
11. 3,000 MT nominal, counterforce only[b,c]	3,000	70	0	1–10	2,150
14. 100 MT nominal, countervalue only[d]	100	0	100	0.1	1,000
16. 5000 MT "severe," counterforce only[b,e]	5,000	100	0	5–10	700
17. 10,000 MT "severe," countervalue and counterforce[d,e]	10,000	63	15	0.1–10	16,160

[a] In the baseline case, 12,000 square kilometers of inner cities are burned; on every square centimeter an average of 10 grams of combustibles are burned, and 1.1% of the burned material rises as smoke. Also, 230,000 square kilometers of suburban areas burn, with 1.5 grams consumed at each square centimeter and 3.6% rising as smoke.

[b] In this highly conservative case, it is assumed that no smoke emission occurs, that not a blade of grass is burned.

[c] Only 25,000 tons of fine dust is raised into the upper atmosphere for every megaton exploded.

[d] In contrast to the baseline case, only inner cities burn, but with 10 grams per square centimeter consumed and 3.3% rising as smoke into the high troposphere.

[e] Here, the fine (submicron) dust raised into the upper atmosphere is 150,000 tons per megaton exploded.

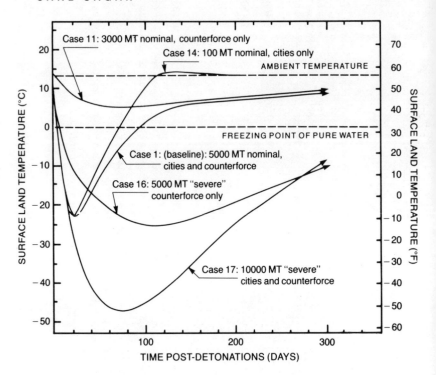

FIGURE 2. In this figure, the average temperature of Northern Hemisphere land areas (away from coastlines) is shown varying with time after a nuclear war. The temperature is shown on the vertical axis, in degrees Centigrade or Celsius at left, and in degrees Fahrenheit at right. The "ambient" temperature is averaged over all latitudes and seasons. Thus normal winter temperatures at north temperate latitudes will be lower than is shown, and normal tropical temperatures will be higher than shown. The upper horizontal dashed line shows the average temperature of the Earth (13° C or 56° F), and the lower dashed horizontal line shows the freezing point of pure water (0° C or 32° F). The horizontal axis measures the time after the nuclear exchange in days from the beginning of the war to almost a year later. Each curve represents a different nuclear war scenario, ranging from 100 megatons (MT) total yield expended in the war to 10,000 MT.

The cases shown here, from a much larger compilation in the TTAPS reports, are described further in table 1. They include a mix of countervalue attacks on industries and cities, in which the main effect is smoke carried to the troposphere from fires, and counterforce attacks on missile silos, in which (very conservatively) no smoke is assumed to be produced but large quantities of dust are injected high into the atmosphere. Cases described as

"nominal" assume the most likely values of parameters (such as dust particle size or the frequency of firestorms) that are imperfectly known. Cases
marked "severe" represent adverse but not implausible values of these parameters. In case 14 the curve ends when the temperatures come within a
degree of the ambient values. For the four other cases, the curves are
shown ending after 300 days, but this is simply because the calculations
were not extended further. In these four cases the curves will continue in the
directions they are headed. Very roughly, case 1 is the sum of cases 11 and
14. Case 16 envisions an exchange that is entirely surface bursts of fairly
high yield designed to destroy silos, and a high percentage of resulting fine
dust. Following is a further description of the five cases:

Case 1 is the TTAPS baseline case in which 4,000 megatons are dedicated
to counterforce attacks by the two sides and 1,000 megatons are allocated
for cities and environs. The main effect is from the soot generated in urban
conflagrations. The temperature minimum of $-23°$ C ($-9°$ F) is reached a
few weeks after the exchange, and temperatures return to the freezing point
after about three months. Recovery to ambient conditions, however, does
not occur for more than a year, because of the slow fallout of stratospheric
dust.

In case 11 the U.S. and/or the S.U. detonate a total of 3,000 megatons on
missile silos and other targets far from cities and forests. Fires are (unreal-
istically) assumed negligible. The land temperatures drop over a period of
three months as fine dust particles are injected into the stratosphere. Since
the dust is removed very slowly from the stratosphere, it takes more than a
year for the temperatures to recover their usual (ambient) values.

In case 14 the exchange is limited to only 100 megatons employed exclusively in low-yield airbursts over cities. In this calculation there is no dust
produced—only smoke from the burning cities, very little of which reaches
the stratosphere. The minimum temperature of $-23°$ C ($-9°$ F) is reached
after a few weeks, and normal temperatures are attained after about 100
days. As the soot settles, sunlight begins to penetrate to the surface. The
soot still suspended in the lower atmosphere traps the heat radiated by the
surface, and for a few months a modest greenhouse effect heats the surface
by a few degrees. One hundred megatons corresponds to about 0.8% of the
strategic nuclear arsenals of the U.S. and S.U.

Case 16 is a 5,000-megaton exchange in which mainly silos are attacked,
in which more fine dust is raised per megaton of yield than in case 11, and
in which there is negligible burning of cities. Here, minimum temperatures
are not reached for four months, when temperatures have dropped to $-25°$
C ($-13°$ F). Because the large amounts of dust emplaced in the stratosphere fall out very slowly, it takes more than a year for the land temperatures to return to the freezing point and much longer than that for normal
temperatures to be reached.

In case 17 about three-fourths of the strategic arsenals of the U.S. and
the S.U. are expended in a mix of attacks on silos and cities. After more
than two months, minimum temperatures of $-47°$ C ($-53°$ F) are reached—
temperatures characteristic of the surace of Mars. The soot falls out comparatively rapidly, and the slowness of the recovery is due to stratospheric dust.
The temperatures return to the freezing point only after about a year.

TABLE 2. Schematic summary of the biological effects of the baseline (5,000 megatons) nuclear war. A schematic representation of the time scale for many of the effects is presented; the effects are most severe when the thickness of the horizontal bar is greatest. "Synergisms" is a potentially significant category in which the total result is greater than the sum of the component effects. Most synergisms are entirely unknown. At right is an indication of the risks to American/Soviet populations, to Northern Hemisphere populations, to Southern Hemisphere populations, and to the entire human community of the various effects listed. H, M, and L stand for high, medium, and low, respectively. In the last column only, L represents zero to a million deaths; M, a million to a few hundred million deaths; and H, more than a few hundred million deaths. (Chart prepared by Mark Harwell and the author.)

Effect	Time After Nuclear War	U.S./S.U. Population at risk	N.H. Population at risk	S.H. Population at risk	Casualty rate for those at risk	Potential global deaths
Blast		H	M	L	H	M-H
Thermal Radiation		H	M	L	M	M-H
Prompt Ionizing Radiation		L	L	L	H	L-M
Fires		M	M	L	M	M
Toxic Gases		M	M	L	L	L
Dark		H	H	M	L	L

Time axis (Time After Nuclear War): 1 hr, 1 day, 1 wk, 1 mo, 3 mo, 6 mo, 1 yr, 2 yr, 5 yr, 10 yr

24

Cold							M-H	H	H	H	H

Cold	M-H	H	H	H	H
Frozen Water Supplies	M	M	M	H	H
Fallout Ionizing Radiation	M-H	M	L-M	H	H
Food Shortages	H	H	H	H	H
Medical System Collapse	M	M	M	H	H
Contagious Diseases	M	H	L	M	M
Epidemics and Pandemics	M	M	M	H	H
Psychiatric Disorders	L-M	L	L	H	H
Increased Surface Ultraviolet Light	L	L	M	H	H
Synergisms	?	?	?	?	?

to recover rather than thousands of years. No new ice age is likely to be induced by the nuclear winter.

Because of the obscuration of the Sun, the daytime light levels can fall to a twilit gloom or worse. For more than a week in the northern mid-latitude target zone, it might be much too dark to see, even at midday. In cases 1 and 14 (table 1) hemispherically averaged light levels fall to a few percent of normal values, comparable to that at the bottom of a dense overcast. At this illumination, many plants are close to what is called the compensation point, the light level at which photosynthesis can barely keep pace with plant metabolism. In case 17, illumination, averaged over the entire Northern Hemisphere, falls in daytime to about 0.1 percent of normal, a light level in which most plants will not photosynthesize at all. For cases 1 and especially 17, full recovery to ordinary daylight takes a year or more (figure 2).

As the fine particles fall out of the atmosphere, carrying radioactivity to the ground, the light levels increase and the surface warms. The depleted ozone layer now permits solar ultraviolet light to reach the Earth's surface in increased proportions. The relative timing of the multitude of adverse consequences of a nuclear war is shown in table 2.

Perhaps the most striking and unexpected consequence of our study is that even a comparatively small nuclear war can have devastating climatic consequences, provided cities are targeted (see case 14 in figure 2; here, the centers of a hundred major NATO and Warsaw Pact cities are burning). There is an indication of a very approximate threshold at which severe climatic consequences are triggered—around a few hundred nuclear explosions over cities, for smoke generation, or around 2,000 to 3,000 high-yield surface bursts at missile silos, for example, for dust generation and ancillary fires. Fine particles can be injected into the atmosphere at increasing rates with only minor effects until these thresholds are crossed. Thereafter, the effects increase rapidly in severity.[6]

6. The climatic threshold for smoke in the troposphere is about 100 million metric tons, injected essentially all at once; for submicron fine dust in

As in all calculations of this complexity, there are uncertainties. Some factors tend to work toward more severe or more prolonged effects; others tend to ameliorate the effects.[7] The detailed TTAPS calculations described here are one-dimensional; that is, they assume the fine particles to move vertically by all the appropriate laws of physics, but neglect the spreading in latitude and longitude. When soot or dust is moved away from the reference locale, things get better there and worse elsewhere. In addition, fine particles can be transported by weather systems to other locales, where they are carried more rapidly down to the surface. This would ameliorate obscuration not only locally but globally. It is just this transport away from northern mid-latitudes that involves the equatorial zone and the Southern Hemisphere in the effects of the nuclear war. It would be helpful to perform an accurate three-dimensional calculation on the general atmospheric circulation following a nuclear war. Preliminary estimates (Turco et al., 1983) suggest that the general circulation might moderate the low-temperature excursions of our calculations by some 30 percent, lessening somewhat the severity of the effects, but still leaving them at catastrophic levels (for example, a 30° C rather than a 40° C temperature drop). To provide a small margin of safety, we neglect this correction in our subsequent discussion.

Then there are holes in the clouds. Very few accessible targets are in the Atlantic and Pacific oceans. If such moving clear patches (an "Atlantic" hole and a "Pacific" hole) were to appear at regular intervals over most places in the Northern Hemisphere, the effects of cold and dark would be somewhat lessened. However, fires set, for example, in western North America or in Eurasian taigas, would continue

the stratosphere, about the same. The existence of a threshold derives from the fact that the attenuation of sunlight depends not linearly, but exponentially, on the quantity of fine particles in the line of sight to the Sun; in simple radiative transfer theory, this is known as Beer's Law.

7. The slow warming of the Earth owing to a CO_2 greenhouse effect attendant to the burning of fossil fuels should not be thought of as tempering the nuclear winter; the greenhouse temperature increments are too small and too slow.

burning, some perhaps for weeks, and new fires will be set: delayed launches may be directed at targets temporarily within a hole to aid satellite verification of target destruction. In addition, the winds at different altitudes move at different velocities, and a patch at one altitude may be over or under a thick cloud layer at another altitude. The dust injected into the stratosphere by the Mexican volcano, El Chichón, in its explosion on April 4, 1982, took ten days to reach Asia and two weeks to reach Africa, and circumnavigated the globe in three weeks—leaving a thin ribbon of particles behind it about 10° of latitude wide. When there are many sources of particles instead of one, the holes will close still faster. For these reasons, it seems unlikely that moving holes would remain unfilled or uncovered for more than a week or two, or that patchiness could ameliorate the climatic effects in a major way.

There are also effects that tend to make the results much worse. For example, in our calculations we assumed that rainout of fine particles occurred through the entire troposphere. But under realistic circumstances, at least the upper troposphere may be very dry, and any dust or soot carried there initially may take much longer to rain out. There is also a very significant effect, deriving from the drastically altered structure of the atmosphere, brought about by the heating of the clouds and the cooling of the surface. This produces a region in which the temperature is approximately constant with altitude in the lower atmosphere and topped by a massive temperature inversion (figures 1b and 1c). Particles throughout the atmosphere would thereafter be transported up or down very slowly—as in the present stratosphere. This is a second reason that the lifetime of the clouds of soot and dust may be much longer than we have calculated. If so, the worst of the cold and the dark might be prolonged for considerable periods of time, conceivably for more than a year. We also neglect this effect in subsequent discussion.

Nuclear war scenarios are possible that are much worse than the ones we have presented. For example, if command and control capabilities are lost early in the war—by, say, "decapitation" (an early surprise attack on civilian and military headquarters and communications facilities)—then the war conceivably could be extended for weeks as local commanders make separate and uncoordinated decisions. At least some of the delayed missile launches could be retaliatory strikes against any remaining adversary cities. Generation of an additional smoke pall over a period of weeks or longer following the initiation of the war would extend the magnitude, but especially the duration, of the climatic consequences. Or it is possible, within the boundaries of plausibility, that more cities and forests would be ignited than we have assumed, or that smoke emissions would be larger, or that a greater fraction of the world arsenals would be committed. Less severe cases, within the same boundaries, are of course possible as well.

These calculations therefore are not, and cannot be, assured prognostications of the full consequences of a nuclear war. Many refinements in them are possible and are being pursued. But there seems to be general agreement on the overall conclusions: in the wake of a nuclear war there is likely to be a period, lasting at least for months, of extreme cold in a radioactive gloom followed—after the soot and dust falls out—by an extended period of increased ultraviolet light reaching the surface.[8]

We now explore the biological impact of such an assault on the global environment.

Biological Consequences

The immediate human consequences of nuclear explosions range from vaporization of populations near the hypocenter, to blast-generated trauma (from flying glass, falling beams, collapsing skyscrapers, and the like), to burns, radiation sickness, shock, and severe psychiatric disorders. But our concern here is with longer term effects (Ehrlich et al., 1983).

8. These results are dependent on important work by a large number of scientists who have previously examined aspects of this subject; many of these workers are acknowledged in Turco et al., 1983.

It is now a commonplace that in the burning of modern tall buildings, more people succumb to toxic gases than to fire. Ignition of many varieties of building materials, insulation, and fabrics generates large amounts of such pyrotoxins, including carbon monoxide, cyanides, vinyl chlorides, oxides of nitrogen, ozone, dioxins, and furans. Because of differing practices in the use of such synthetics, the burning of cities in North America and Western Europe will probably generate more pyrotoxins than cities in the Soviet Union, and cities with substantial recent construction more than older unreconstructed cities. In nuclear war scenarios in which a great many cities are burning, a significant pyrotoxin smog might persist for months. The magnitude of this danger is unknown.

The pyrotoxins, low light levels, radioactive fallout, subsequent ultraviolet light, and especially the cold are together likely to destroy almost all of Northern Hemisphere agriculture, even for the more modest cases 11 and 14. A 12° to 15° C temperature reduction by itself would eliminate wheat and corn production in the United States, even if all civil systems and agricultural technology were intact (Pimentel & Sorrells, 1983). With unavoidable societal disruption, and with the other environmental stresses just mentioned, even a 3,000-megaton "pure" counterforce attack (case 11) might suffice. Realistically, many fires would be set even in such an attack (see below), and a 3,000-megaton war is likely to wipe out U.S. grain production. This would represent by itself an unprecedented global catastrophe: North American grain is the principal reliable source of export food on the planet, as well as an essential component of U.S. prosperity. Wars just before harvesting of grain and other staples would be incrementally worse than wars after harvesting. For many scenarios, the effects will extend (see figure 2) into two or more growing seasons. Widespread fires and subsequent runoff of topsoil are among the many additional deleterious consequences extending for years after the war.

Something like three-quarters of the U.S. population lives in or near cities. In the cities themselves there is, on average, only about one week's supply of food. After a nuclear war, it is conceivable that enough of present grain storage might survive to maintain on some level the present population for more than a year (provided storage facilities are not targeted). But with the breakdown of civil order and transportation systems in the cold, the dark, and the fallout, these stores would become largely inaccessible. Vast numbers of survivors, if they did not freeze to death, would soon starve to death.

In addition, the subfreezing temperatures imply, in many cases, the unavailability of fresh water. The ground will tend to be frozen to a depth of about a meter—incidentally making it unlikely that the hundreds of millions of dead bodies would be buried, even if the civil organization to do so existed. Fuel stores to melt snow and ice would be in short supply, and ice surfaces and freshly fallen snow would tend to be contaminated by radioactivity and pyrotoxins.

In the presence of excellent medical care, the average value of the acute lethal dose of ionizing radiation for healthy adults is about 450 rads. (As with many other effects, children, the infirm, and the elderly tend to be more vulnerable.) Combined with the other assaults on survivors in the postwar environment, and in the probable absence of any significant medical care, the mean lethal acute dose is likely to decline to 350 rads or even lower. For many outdoor scenarios, doses within the fallout plumes that drift hundreds of kilometers downwind of targets are greater than the mean lethal dose. (For a 10,000-megaton war, this is true for more than 30 percent of northern mid-latitude land areas.) Far from targets, intermediate-time-scale chronic doses from delayed radioactive fallout may be in excess of 100 rads for the baseline case. These calculations assume no detonations on nuclear reactors or fuel reprocessing plants, which would increase the dose.

Thus, the combination of acute doses from prompt radioacive fallout, chronic doses from the delayed intermediate-time-scale fallout, and internal doses from food and drink are together likely to kill many more by radiation sickness.

Because of acute damage to bone marrow, survivors would have significantly increased vulnerability to infectious diseases. Most infants exposed to 100 rads as fetuses in the first two trimesters of pregnancy would suffer mental retardation and/or other serious birth defects. Radiation and some pyrotoxins would later produce neoplastic diseases and genetic damage. Livestock and domesticated animals, with fewer resources, vanishing food supplies, and in many cases greater sensitivity to the stresses of nuclear war than human beings, would also perish in large numbers.

These devastating consequences for humans and for agriculture would not be restricted to the locales in which the war would principally be "fought," but would extend throughout northern mid-latitudes and, with reduced but still significant severity, probably to the tropics and the Southern Hemisphere. The bulk of the world's grain exports originate in northern mid-latitudes. Many nations in the developed as well as the developing world depend on the import of food. Japan, for example, imports 75 percent of its food (and 99 percent of its fuel). Even if there were no climatic and radiation stresses on tropical and Southern Hemisphere societies—many of them already at subsistence levels of nutrition—large numbers of people there would die of starvation.

As agriculture breaks down worldwide (possible initial exceptions might include Argentina, Australia, and South Africa if the climatic impact on the Southern Hemisphere proved to be minimal), there will be increasing reliance on natural ecosystems—fruits, tubers, roots, nuts, and so on. But wild foodstuffs will also have suffered from the effects of the war. At just the moment that surviving humans turn to the natural environment for the basis of life, that environment would be experiencing a devastation unprecedented in recent geological history.

Two-thirds of all species of plants, animals, and microorganisms on Earth live within 25° of the equator. Because temperatures tend to vary with the seasons only minimally at tropical latitudes, species there are especially vulnerable to rapid temperature declines. In past major extinction events in the paleontological record, there has been a marked tendency for tropical organisms to show greater vulnerability than organisms living at more temperate latitudes. The darkness alone may cause a collapse in the aquatic food chain in which sunlight is harvested by phytoplankton, phytoplankton by zooplankton, zooplankton by small fish, small fish by large fish, and, occasionally, large fish by humans. In many nuclear war scenarios this food chain is likely to collapse at its base for at least a year and is significantly more imperiled in tropical waters. The increase in ultraviolet light available at the surface of the earth approximately a year after the war provides an additional major environmental stress that by itself has been described as having "profound consequences" for aquatic, terrestrial, and other ecosystems (Kruger et al., 1982).

The global ecosystem can be considered an intricately woven fabric composed of threads contributed by the millions of separate species that inhabit the planet and interact with the air, the water, and the soil. The system has developed considerable resiliency, so that pulling a single thread is unlikely to unravel the entire fabric. Thus, most ordinary assaults on the biosphere do not have catastrophic consequences. For example, because of natural small changes in stratospheric ozone abundance, organisms have probably experienced, in the fairly recent geological past, 10 percent fluctuations in the solar near-ultraviolet flux (but not fluctuations by factors of 2 or more). Similarly, small temperature variations routinely occur, but major continental temperature changes of the magnitude and extent addressed here may not have been experienced for thousands and possibly not for tens of millions of years. We have no experimental information, even for aquaria or terraria, on the simultaneous effects of cold, dark, pyrotoxins, ionizing radiation, and ultraviolet light as predicted in the TTAPS study.[9]

Each of these factors, taken separately, may carry serious

9. Such simulations, especially on fairly large-scale ecological systems, represent a possibly important field for future research.

consequences for the global ecosystem: their interactions may be much more dire still. Extremely worrisome is the possibility of poorly understood or as yet entirely uncontemplated synergisms (where the net consequences of two or more assaults on the environment is much more than the sum of the component parts). For example, as mentioned above, more than 100 rads (and possibly more than 200 rads) of external and ingested ionizing radiation is likely to be delivered in a very large nuclear war to all plants, animals, and unprotected humans in densely populated regions of northern mid-latitudes. After the soot and dust clears, there can also be for such wars a 200 to 400 percent increment in the solar ultraviolet flux that reaches the ground, with an increase of many orders of magnitude in the more dangerous shorter wavelength radiation. Together, these radiation assaults are likely to suppress the immune system of humans and other species, making them more vulnerable to disease. At the same time, the high ambient radiation fluxes are likely to produce, through mutation, new varieties of microorganisms, some of which might become pathogenic. The preferential radiation sensitivity of birds and other insect predators would enhance the proliferation of herbivorous and pathogen-carrying insects. Carried by vectors with high radiation tolerance, it seems possible that epidemics and global pandemics would propagate with no hope of effective mitigation by medical care, even with reduced population sizes and greatly restricted human mobility. Plants, weakened by low temperatures and low light levels, and animals, would likewise be vulnerable to preexisting and newly arisen pathogens.

There are many other conceivable synergisms, all of them still poorly understood because of the complexity of the global ecosystem. Every synergism represents an additional assault, of unknown magnitude, on the global ecosystem and its support functions for humans. What the world would look like after a nuclear war depends in part upon the unknown synergistic interaction of the various adverse effects (figure 3).

We do not and cannot know that the worst would happen after a nuclear war. Perhaps there is some as yet undiscovered compensating effect or saving grace—although in the past the overlooked effects in studies of nuclear war have almost always tended toward the worst. But in an uncertain matter of such gravity, it is wise to contemplate the worst, especially when its probability is not extremely small. The summary of the findings of the group of forty distinguished biologists who met in April 1983 to assess the TTAPS conclusions is worthy of careful consideration:

> Species extinction could be expected for most tropical plants and animals, and for most terrestrial vertebrates of north temperate regions, a large number of plants, and numerous freshwater and some marine organisms. . . . Whether any people would be able to persist for long in the face of highly modified biological communities; novel climates; high levels of radiation; shattered agricultural, social, and economic systems; extraordinary psychological stresses; and a host of other difficulties is open to question. It is clear that the ecosystem effects *alone* resulting from a large-scale thermonuclear war could be enough to destroy the current civilization in at least the Northern Hemisphere. Coupled with the direct casualties of over 1 billion people, the combined intermediate and long-term effects of nuclear war suggest that eventually there might be no human survivors in the Northern Hemisphere.
>
> Furthermore, the scenario described here is by no means the most severe that could be imagined with present world nuclear arsenals and those contemplated for the near future (TTAPS). In almost any large-scale nuclear exchange between the superpowers, global environmental changes sufficient to cause the extinction of a major fraction of the plant and animal species on Earth is likely. In that event, the possibility of the extinction of *Homo sapiens* cannot be excluded. (Ehrlich et al., 1983)

Doctrine and Policy Implications

The foregoing probable consequences of various nuclear war scenarios have implications for doctrine and policy. Some, their capacity for horror perhaps exhausted, have argued that the difference between the deaths of several hundred million people in a nuclear war (as has been thought until recently to be a reasonable upper limit) and the death of every person on Earth (as now seems possible) is only a matter of one order of magnitude. For me, the difference is considerably greater. Restricting our attention only to those who die as a consequence of the war conceals its full impact. If we are required to calibrate extinction in numerical terms, I would be sure to include the number of people in future generations who would not be born. A nuclear war imperils all our descendants, for as long as there will be humans. Even if the population remains static, with an average lifetime of the order of a hundred years, over a typical time period for the biological evolution of a successful species (roughly 10 million years), we are talking about some 500 trillion people yet to come. By this criterion, the stakes are 1 million times greater for extinction than for the more modest nuclear wars that kill "only" hundreds of millions of people. There are many other possible measures of the potential loss—including culture and science, the evolutionary history of the planet, and the significance of the lives of all our ancestors who contributed to the future of their descendants. Extinction is the undoing of the human enterprise.

The new results on climatic catastrophe seem to raise the stakes of nuclear war enormously. But I recognize that there are those, including some policymakers, who feel that the increased level of fatalities and the prospect of extinction have little impact on policy, but who nevertheless acknowledge that the newly emerging consequences of nuclear war may require changes in specific points of strategic doctrine. I here set down what seem to me some of the more apparent implications, within the context of present nuclear stockpiles. The idea of a crude threshold, very roughly around 500 to 2,000 contemporary warheads, for triggering the climatic catastrophe will be central to some of these considerations. (Such a threshold applies only to something like the present distribution of yields in the strategic arsenals. Drastic conversion to very low-yield weapons—see below—changes some of the picture dramatically.) I hope others will critically and constructively examine these preliminary thoughts and explore additional implications of the TTAPS results.

First Strike

The MIRVing of missiles (that is, the introduction of multiple warheads), improvements in accuracy, and other developments have increased the perceived temptation to launch a devastating first strike against land targets—even though both sides retain a powerful retaliatory force in airborne bombers and submarines at sea. Much current concern and national rhetoric is addressed to the first-strike capability of extant or proposed weapons systems. The mere capability of a first strike creates incentives for a preemptive attack. Launch-on-warning and simultaneous release of all strategic weapons are two of several ominous and destabilizing innovations contrived in response to the fear of a first strike.

The number of U.S. land-based strategic missiles is about 1,050; for the S.U., about 1,400. In addition, each side has at least several dozen dedicated and alternative strategic bomber bases and airstrips, as well as command and control facilities, submarine ports, and other prime strategic targets on land. Each target requires—for high probability of its destruction—two or perhaps three attacking warheads. Thus, a convincing first strike against land targets requires at least 2,200 and perhaps as many as 4,500 attacking warheads. Some—for example, those intended to disable bombers that succeed in becoming airborne just before the first strike—would detonate as airbursts. While many missile silos, especially in the U.S., are surrounded by farmland and brush, other strategic targets, especially in Europe and Asia, are sufficiently near forests or urban areas for major conflagrations to be set, even in a "pure" counterforce attack. Accordingly, a major first strike would be clearly in the vicinity of, and perhaps well over, the climatic threshold.

Moreover, a counterforce first strike is unlikely to be entirely effective. Perhaps 10 to 40 percent of the adversary's silos and most of its airborne bombers and submarines at sea will survive, and *its* response may be not against silos, but against cities. Ten percent of a 5,000-warhead strategic arsenal is 500 warheads: distributed over cities, this seems by itself enough to trigger a major climatic catastrophe.

Such a first-strike scenario, in which the danger to the aggressor nation depends upon the unpredictable response of the attacked nation, seems risky enough. (The hope for the aggressor nation is that its retained second-strike force, largely strategic submarines and unlaunched land-based missiles, will intimidate the adversary into surrender rather than provoke it into retaliation.) But the decision to launch a first strike, which is tantamount to national suicide for the aggressor even if the attacked nation does not lift a finger to retaliate, is a different circumstance altogether. If a first strike gains no more than a pyrrhic victory of ten days' duration before the prevailing winds carry the nuclear winter to the aggressor nation, the "attractiveness" of the first strike would seem to be diminished significantly.

A Doomsday Machine[10] is useless if the potential adversary is ignorant of its presence. But since many distinguished scientists, both American and Soviet, have participated vigorously in recent studies of the climatic consequences of nuclear war, since there appears to be no significant disagreement in the conclusions, and since policymakers will doubtless be apprised of these new results, it would appear that a decision to launch a major first strike is now much less rational and therefore, perhaps, much less probable. (Such conclusions are more secure the better political leaders understand the nuclear winter.) If true, this should have cascading consequences for specific weapons systems.

The perceived vulnerability to a first strike has been a major source of stress and fear and thereby a major spur to the nuclear arms race. Knowledge that a first strike is now less

10. For the term "Doomsday Machine," I am indebted to Herman Kahn, *On Thermonuclear War* (Princeton: Princeton University Press, 1960).

probable might make at least some small contribution to dissipating the poisonous atmosphere of mistrust that currently characterizes U.S./S.U. relations.

Subthreshold War

Devastating nuclear wars that are nevertheless significantly below the threshold for severe climatic consequences certainly seem possible—for example, the destruction of ten or twenty cities, or a hundred silos of a particularly destabilizing missile system. Nevertheless, might some nation be tempted to initiate or engage in a much larger, but still reliably subthreshold nuclear war? The hope might be that the attacked adversary would be reluctant to retaliate for fear of crossing the threshold. This is not very different from the hope that a counterforce first strike would not be followed by a retaliatory strike, because of the aggressor's retention of an invulnerable (for example, submarine-based) second-strike force adequate to destroy populations and national economies. It suffers the same deficiency—profound uncertainty about the likely response.

The strategic forces of the U.S. or the S.U.—even if they were all at fixed sites—could not be destroyed in a reliably subthreshold war: there are too many essential targets. Thus, a subthreshold first strike powerfully provokes the attacked nation and leaves much of its retaliatory force untouched. It is easy to imagine a nation, having contemplated becoming the object of a subthreshold first strike, planning to respond in kind because it judges that failure to do so would itself invite attack. Retaliation could occur immediately against a few key cities—if national leaders were restrained and command and control facilities intact—or massively, months later, after much of the dust and smoke have fallen out, extending the duration but ameliorating the severity of the net climatic effects.

However, this may not be the case for such nations as Britain, France, or China. Because of the marked contiguity of strategic targets and urban areas in Europe, the climatic threshold for attacks on European nuclear powers may be significantly less than for the U.S. or S.U. Nevertheless, provided it could be accomplished without triggering a U.S./S.U. nuclear war, first strikes against all the fixed-site strategic forces of one of these nations might not trigger the climatic catastrophe. The invulnerable retaliatory capability of these nations, however—especially the ballistic missile submarines of Britain and France—makes such a first strike unlikely.

Treaties on Yields and Targeting

I would not include this possibility, except that it has been mentioned publicly by Edward Teller. The proposal has two parts. The first is to ban by treaty all nuclear warheads with yields in excess of 300 or 400 kilotons. The fireballs from warheads of higher yields mainly penetrate into the stratosphere and work to deplete the ozonosphere. The reconversion of nuclear warheads to lower individual yields would reduce (although not remove) the threat of significantly enhanced ultraviolet radiation at the surface of the Earth, but would in itself have no bearing on the issue of climatic catastrophe and would increase the intermediate-time-scale radioactive fallout. With the present strategic arsenals, there is no mix of yields that simultaneously minimizes ionizing radiation from fallout and ultraviolet radiation from the Sun. As delivery system accuracy has progressively improved, there has been a corresponding tendency toward the deployment of lower yield warheads, although not through any concern about the integrity of the ozonosphere. There is also a trend toward higher fission fractions, implying more radioactive fallout. Limitations on the sizes and therefore to some extent on the yields of new warheads is part of recent U.S. arms control proposals. However, with the bulk of S.U. strategic warheads having yields larger than their U.S. counterparts, treaties limiting high yields place greater demands on S.U. than on U.S. compliance. Moreover, to enforce a categorical yield ceiling seems to imply verification problems of some difficulty.

The second part of the proposal is to guarantee by treaty that cities would not be targeted. Then, the worst of the climatic effects might be avoided, although climatic consequences of "pure" counterforce exchanges can still be extremely serious (figure 2). However, targeting coordinate encoding is in principle done remotely and involves different coordinates for each warhead. Even if we could imagine international inspection teams descending unannounced on Soviet or American missile silos to inspect the targeting coordinates, an hour later the coordinates could be returned to those appropriate for cities. Targeting policy is among the most sensitive aspects of nuclear strategy, and maintaining uncertainty about targeting policy is thought to be an essential component of deterrence. The proposal is unlikely to be received warmly by the Joint Strategic Targeting Staff or its Soviet counterpart. It is also difficult to understand how those skeptical of the verifiability by reconnaissance satellites of SALT II provisions on the deployment of missiles 10 meters long can rest easy about verification of treaties controlling what is encoded in a microchip 1 millimeter long. Nevertheless, a symbolic, unverifiable targeting treaty, entered into because both sides recognize that it is not in their interest to target cities, might have some merit.

Transition to Low-Yield High-Accuracy Warheads

A conceivable response to the prospect of climatic catastrophe might be to continue present trends toward lower yield and higher accuracy missiles, perhaps accompanied by development of the technology for warheads to burrow subsurface before detonating. Payloads have been developed for the Pershing 2 missile that use radar area correlators for target recognition and terminal guidance; the targeting probable error is said to be 40 meters (120 feet) (*Aviation Week and Space Technology*, 1979). It is evident that a technology is gradually emerging that could permit delivery accuracies of 35 meters or better over intercontinental ranges. It is evident as well that burrowing technology is also under rapid development. A 1-kiloton burst, 2 to 3 meters subsurface, will excavate a crater roughly 60 meters across (Glasstone & Dolan, 1977). Clearly, high-accuracy penetrating warheads in the 1-to-10-kiloton range would be able, with high reliability, to destroy even very hardened silos and underground command posts. Low-yield subsurface explosions of this sort cannot threaten the ozonosphere. They minimize fires, soot, stratospheric dust, and radioactive fallout. Even several thousand simultaneous such detonations might not trigger the nuclear winter. Similar technology might be used for pinpoint attacks on military-industrial targets in urban areas. Thus, the TTAPS results will probably lead to calls for further improvements in high-accuracy earth-burrowing warheads.

There are, I think, a number of difficulties with this proposal, as attractive as it seems in a strictly military context. A world in which the nuclear arsenals were completely converted to a relatively small number of burrowing low-yield warheads would be much safer in terms of the climatic catastrophe. But such warheads are provocative. They are the perfect post-TTAPS first-strike weapon. Their development might well be taken as a serious interest in eventually making a climatically safe but disabling first strike. Greatly expanded deployment of antiballistic missiles might be one consequence of their buildup. Retaliation from surviving silos, aircraft, and, especially, submarines, as discussed above, is likely, whatever the disposition of yields in a first strike. Also, arsenals cannot be converted instantaneously. There would thus be a dangerous and protracted transition period in which enough newer weapons are deployed to be destabilizing and enough older weapons are still in place to trigger the nuclear winter.

However, if the inventories of modern higher yield warheads (more than 10 kilotons) were first brought below threshold, a coordinated U.S./S.U. deployment of low-yield burrowers might be accomplished in somewhat greater safety. On many launchers, each with a single warhead, they might provide a useful reassurance to defense ministries at some points in the transition process. At any rate, the dramatic reduction of arsenals necessary to go below threshold before

large-scale burrower deployment is indistinguishable from
major arms reduction for its own sake (see below).

Consequences for the Developing World

Before the TTAPS calculations were performed, it was possible to argue that the developing world would be severely
affected by secondary economic consequences, but not fundamentally destroyed by a northern mid-latitude nuclear war.
Now it seems more likely that nations having no part in the
conflict—even nations entirely neutral in the global confrontation between the U.S. and the S.U.—might be reduced to
prehistoric population levels and economies, or worse. Nations between 70° N and 30° S, nations with marginal economies, nations with large food imports or extensive malnu-
trition today, and nations with their own strategic targets are
particularly at risk. The very survival of nations distant from
any likely nuclear conflict depends on the prudence and wisdom of the major nuclear powers. India, Brazil, Nigeria, or
Saudi Arabia could collapse in a nuclear war without a single
bomb being dropped on their territories.[11] Quite apart from
any concern about the deflection of world financial, technical, and intellectual resources to the nuclear arms race, the
prospect of nuclear war threatens every nation and every
person on the planet. The diplomatic and economic pressure accordingly placed on the five nuclear powers by the
other nations of the world, concerned about their own survival, could be at least marginally significant.

11. The distribution of the coldest regions will vary with time and to-
pography. In one recent but very crude three-dimensional simulation of the
baseline nuclear winter, by forty days after the war the temperature has
dropped 15–40° centigrade over a vast region extending from Chad to No-
vosibirsk, from the Caspian Sea to Sri Lanka, embracing India, Pakistan, and
western China, and having its most severe effects in Afghanistan, Iran, and
Saudi Arabia (V. V. Alexandrov and G. L. Stenchikov, preprint, Computing
Center, USSR Academy of Sciences, Moscow, 1983.)

Shelters

The usual sorts of shelters envisioned for civilian populations are ineffective even for the nuclear war consequences known before the TTAPS study. The more ambitious among them include food and water for a week or two, modest heating capabilities, rudimentary sanitary and air filtration facilities, and no provisions for the psychological burdens of an extended stay below ground with unknown climatic and ecological consequences propagating overhead. The kinds of shelters suitable for prolonged subfreezing temperatures, high radiation doses, and pyrotoxins would have to be very much more elaborate—quite apart from the question of what good it would be to emerge six or nine months later to an ultra-violet-bathed and biologically depauperate surface, with insect pests proliferating, disease rampant, and the basis of agriculture destroyed. Appropriate shelters, able to service individual families or family groups for months to a year, are too expensive for most families even in the affluent West. The construction of major government shelters for civilian populations would be enormously expensive as well as in itself potentially destabilizing. The prospect of the climatic catastrophe also heightens the perceived inequity between government leaders and (in some cases) their families, provided elaborate shelters, and the bulk of the civilian population, unable to afford even a minimally adequate shelter. But even if it were possible to build perfectly effective shelters for the entire populations of the U.S. and the S.U., this would in no way address the danger to which the rest of the world would be put. Shelters for the combatant nations under circumstances in which only their citizens are threatened is one thing. Shelters for the combatant nations when gravely threatened noncombatant nations have only rudimentary or nonexistent shelters is a very different matter.

Ballistic Missile Defense Systems

It might be argued that the prospect of a climatic catastrophe strengthens whatever arguments there may be for ground-based or space-based ballistic missile defense (BMD) systems, as proposed by the president of the United States in his March 23, 1983, "Star Wars" speech. There are grave technical, cost, and policy difficulties with such proposals (Garwin, 1983; Bethe et al., 1984; Tirman, 1984; Carter, 1984; Drell et al., 1984). Even advocates do not envision it being fully operational in less than two or three decades. Even optimistic informed estimates of porosity or "penetrance" (the fraction of attacking missiles successfully detonating at their targets despite the BMD) are no lower than 5 to 30 percent. The present world arsenal of strategic warheads is so much greater than the threshold for climatic catastrophe that, even if 5 to 30 percent of attacking missiles get through in something like a full exchange, the catastrophe could be triggered. And most competent estimates put the porosity—at least for the foreseeable future—at 50 to 99 percent. Further, one likely response to an adversary's anticipated deployment of BMD systems would be a proportionate increase in the stockpiles of offensive warheads in compensation.

There are three phases in the trajectories of incoming missiles during which they might be attacked: boost phase, midcourse phase, and terminal phase. Boost phase and midcourse interception would, at best, require an untried technology deployed at scales never before attempted. Only terminal phase BMDs exist at the present time (antiballistic missiles, ABMs), and even they, ineffective as they are, may require ruinous capital investments before they can provide meaningful levels of defense. Developments in terminal phase maneuverability of attacking warheads are likely to raise the price tag of an effective BMD sharply again. Even in the best of circumstances, offense will be more effective and less costly than defense.

But terminal phase interception, generally effective only for hard-target defense, characteristically occurs at very low altitudes. There is an advantage to the offense if it fuses the incoming missiles so they will explode if attacked ("sympathetic detonation"). In some schemes, the BMD itself involves nuclear warheads exploded near the ground. A fair fraction of hard targets, especially in Europe and the S.U., are within a few tens of kilometers of cities or forests. Thus the most readily deployable BMD suffers the disability, when it works at all, of generating fires contributory to a climatic catastrophe, quite apart from its porosity. For the foreseeable future, BMD systems cannot prevent the nuclear winter.

Other Possibilities

There are a number of other conceivable responses to the climatic catastrophe, some even more desperate than those discussed above. For example, a nation might relocate its silos and mobile launchers (the latter inviting barrage attack) to cities and forests to guarantee that a barely adequate counterforce first strike by its adversary would trigger a global climatic catastrophe with high confidence. Or nations with small nuclear arsenals or marginal strategic capability might contemplate amassing a threshold arsenal of some 500 to 2,000 contemporary deliverable warheads in order to be taken seriously in "great-power" politics. But these and similar contrivances increase the probability of nuclear war or the dangers attendant to nuclear war sufficiently that they are likely to be rejected by the nation contemplating such moves or, failing that, by other nations. Major relocations of strategic weapons systems or the deployment of new strategic arsenals are readily detectable by national technical means.

None of the foregoing possible strategic and policy responses to the prospect of a nuclear war-triggered climatic catastrophe seems adequate even for the security of the nuclear powers, much less for the rest of the world. The prospect reinforces, in the short run, the standard arguments for strategic confidence building, especially between the U.S. and the S.U.; for tempering puerile rhetoric; for resisting the temptation to demonize the adversary; for reducing the likelihood of strategic confrontations arising from accident or miscalculation; for stabilizing old and new weapons systems—for example, by de-MIRVing missiles; for abandoning nuclear war fighting strategies and mistrusting the possibility of "containment" of a tactical or limited nuclear war; for considering safe unilateral steps such as the retiring of some old weapons systems with very high-yield warheads; for guaranteeing that the highly destabilizing introduction of space weapons be prevented; for improving communications at all levels, especially among general staffs and between heads of government; and for public declarations of relevant policy changes. The U.S. might also contemplate ratification of the 1948 UN Convention on the Prevention and Punishment of the Crime of Genocide (ratified by ninety-two nations, including the S.U.).

Both nations might consider abandoning apocalyptic threats and doctrines. To the extent that they are not credible, they undermine deterrence; to the extent that they are credible, they set in motion events that tend toward apocalyptic conclusions.

In the long run, the prospect of climatic catastrophe raises real questions about what is meant by national and international security. To me, it seems clear that the species is in grave danger at least until the world arsenals are reduced below the threshold for climatic catastrophe; the nations and the global civilization would remain vulnerable even at much lower inventories still. It may even be that, now, the only credible arsenal is below threshold. George Kennan's celebrated proposal (Kennan, 1981)[12] to reduce the world arsenals initially to 50 percent of their current numbers is recognized as hard enough to implement. But it would be only the first step toward what is now clearly and urgently needed—a more than 90 percent reduction (Kennan proposed an ultimate reduction of more than 84 percent)—adequate for strategic deterrence, if that is considered essential, but unlikely to trigger the nuclear winter. Still further reductions could then be contemplated.

The detonation of weapons stockpiles near or above threshold would be, we can now recognize, in contravention of the 1977 Geneva Convention on the Hostile Use of Envi-

12. This was Kennan's acceptance speech for the Albert Einstein Peace Prize, awarded on May 19, 1981, in Washington, D.C.

ronmental Modification Techniques, signed by forty-eight nations and duly ratified by the S.U. and the U.S.[13] Article 6 of the 1968 Nuclear Non-Proliferation Treaty requires the U.S. and the S.U., among other signatory states, "to pursue negotiations in good faith on effective measures relating to cessation of the nuclear arms race at an early date and to nuclear disarmament." I do not imagine that these treaties can, by themselves, play a determining role in producing major reductions in the world strategic arsenals, but they establish some sense of international obligation and can at least expedite urgent bilateral and multilateral consultations.

Reversing the Nuclear Arms Race

We have, in slow and imperceptible steps, been constructing a Doomsday Machine. Until recently—and then, only by accident—no one even noticed. And we have distributed the triggers all over the Northern Hemisphere. Every American and Soviet leader since 1945 has made critical decisions regarding nuclear war in total ignorance of the climatic catastrophe. Perhaps this knowledge would have moderated the subsequent course of world events and, especially, the nuclear arms race. Today, at least, we have no excuse for failing to factor the catastrophe into long-term decisions on strategic policy.

Since it is the soot produced by urban fires that is the most sensitive trigger of the climatic catastrophe, and since such fires can be ignited even by low-yield strategic weapons, it appears that the most critical ready index of the world nuclear arsenals for climatic change may be the total *number* of strategic warheads. (There is some dependence on yield, to

13. Article 1, paragraph 1, states: "Each State Party to this Convention undertakes not to engage in military or any other hostile use of environmental modification techniques having widespread, long-lasting or severe effects as the means of destruction, damage, or injury to another State Party." Paragraph 2 goes on: "Each State Party to this Convention undertakes not to assist, encourage or induce any State, group of States or international organization to engage in activities contrary to the provisions of paragraph 1.

be sure, and future very low-yield high-accuracy burrowing warheads could destroy strategic targets without triggering the nuclear winter, as discussed above.) For other purposes there are other indices—number of submarine-launched warheads, throw weight (net payload deliverable to target), total megatonnage, and so on. From different choices of such indices, different conclusions about strategic parity can be drawn. For total number of strategic warheads, however, the U.S. is "ahead" of the S.U. and always has been.

Traditional belief and childhood experience teach that more weapons buy more security. But since the advent of nuclear weapons and the acquisition of a capacity for over-kill, the possibility has arisen that, past a certain point, more nuclear weapons do not increase national security. I wish here to suggest that, beyond the climatic threshold, an increase in the number of strategic weapons leads to a pronounced *decline* in national (and global) security. These three cases are diagrammed in figure 3. National security is not a zero-sum game. Strategic insecurity of one adversary almost always means strategic insecurity for the other. Conventional pre-1945 wisdom, no matter how deeply felt, is not an adequate guide in an age of apocalyptic weapons.

Very roughly, the level of the world strategic arsenals adequate to induce the climatic catastrophe seems to be somewhere around 500 to 2,000 warheads—an estimate that may be somewhat high for airbursts over cities and somewhat low for high-yield groundbursts. The intrinsic uncertainty in this number is itself of strategic importance, and prudent policy would assume a value below the low end of the plausible range. National or global inventories above this threshold (figure 4) move the world arsenals into a region that might be called the "doomsday zone." If the world's arsenals were well below this rough threshold, no concatenation of computer malfunction, carelessness, unauthorized acts, communications failure, miscalculation, and madness in high office could unleash the nuclear winter. When global arsenals are above this threshold, such a catastrophe is at least possible. The further above threshold we are, the more likely it is that

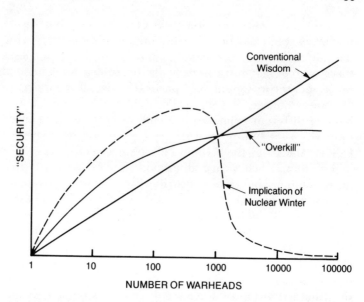

FIGURE 3. Schematic diagram representing, for three different perceptions, the dependence of national "security" (vertical axis) on strategic arsenals (horizontal axis, where each tick mark represents ten times more weapons than the last). In the conventional wisdom, security increases indefinitely
as the number of weapons increases. The curve marked "overkill" reflects a
kind of saturation: when there are enough weapons to destroy any adversary reliably, further weapons purchase no more security. But the TTAPS results suggest that after a threshold of around 500 to 2,000 contemporary
weapons, national security steeply declines with increasing arsenals.

a major exchange would trigger the climatic catastrophe.

If we are content with world inventories above threshold,
we are saying that it is safe to trust the fate of our global civilization and perhaps our species to all leaders, civilian and
military, of all present and future major nuclear powers and
to the command and control efficiency and technical reliability in those nations now and in the indefinite future. For
myself, I would far rather have a world in which the climatic
catastrophe cannot happen, independent of the vicissitudes
of leaders, institutions, and machines. This seems to me elementary planetary hygiene, as well as elementary patriotism.

Something like a thousand warheads (or a few hundred megatons) is of the same order as the arsenals that were publicly announced in the 1950s and 1960s as an unmistakable strategic deterrent and as sufficient to destroy the U.S. or the S.U. "irrecoverably." Considerably smaller arsenals would, with present improvements in accuracy and reliability, probably suffice. Thus it is possible to contemplate a world in which the global strategic arsenals are below threshold, where mutual deterrence is in effect to discourage the use of those surviving warheads, and where, in the unhappy event that some warheads are detonated, there is little likelihood of the climatic catastrophe.[14]

To achieve so dramatic a decline in the global arsenals will require not only heroic measures by both the U.S. and the S.U.—it will also require consistent action by Britain, France, and China, especially when the U.S./S.U. inventories are significantly reduced. Currently proposed increments in the arsenals at least of France would bring that nation's warhead inventory near or above threshold. I have already remarked on the strategic instability, in the context of the climatic catastrophe only, of the warhead inventories of these nations. But if major cuts in the U.S./S.U. arsenals were underway, it is not too much to hope that the other major powers would, after negotiations, follow suit. These considerations also underscore the danger of nuclear weapons proliferation to other nations, especially when the major arsenals are in steep decline.

Figure 4 illustrates the growth of the American and Soviet strategic inventories from 1945 to the present. To minimize confusion in the figure, the British, French, and Chinese arsenals are not shown; they are, however, as just mentioned, significant on the new scale of climatically endangering arsenals. We see from the figure that the U.S. passed the doomsday threshold around 1953 and the S.U. not until about

14. Since higher yield tactical warheads can also be used to burn cities and might do so inadvertently, especially in Europe, provision for their elimination should also eventually be made. But initial attention should be directed to strategic warheads and their delivery systems.

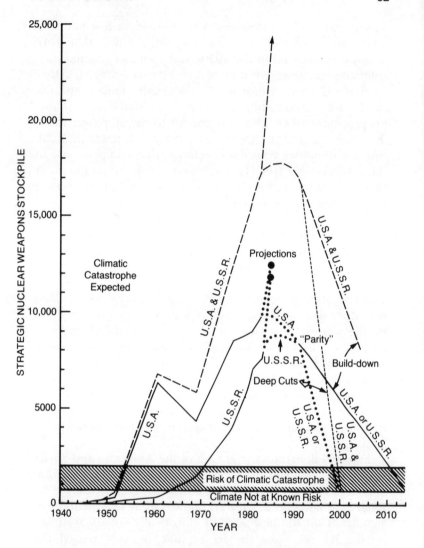

FIGURE 4. The past and future of the strategic (and theater) nuclear arms race. Three regions are shown in the diagram: a lower region at which the nuclear winter could not be triggered, an upper region in which it almost certainly could be triggered ("doomsday zone"), and a transition region, shown shaded. The boundaries of this region are more uncertain than shown and

1966. The largest disparity in the arsenals was in 1961 (a difference of some 6,000 warheads). At the present time the disparity is less than it has been in any year since 1955. A published extrapolation of the present strategic arsenals into 1985 is shown as dashed nearly vertical lines, accommodating new U.S. (Pershing 2, Cruise, MX, and Trident) and S.U. (SS-21, 22, 23) strategic and theater systems. If these projections are valid, the U.S. and the S.U. would have almost identical inventories by the late 1980s.

The uppermost (dash-dot) curve in figure 4 shows the total U.S. and S.U. arsenals (essentially the world arsenals) climbing upward since about 1970 with a very steep slope, the slope steepening still more if the projection is valid. Such exponential or near-exponential runaways are expected in arms races where each side's rate of growth is proportional to its perception of the adversary's weapons inventory; but it is likewise clear that such rapid growth cannot continue in-

depend, among other things, on targeting strategy. But the threshold probably lies between several hundred and a few thousand contemporary strategic weapons.

Between 1945 and the present, the growth of American and Soviet stockpiles is shown as the dark solid lines. The alternating dots and dashes show the sum of these two arsenals, which is also close to the total world arsenals. Although the distinction between tactical weapons and strategic or theater weapons is beginning to be blurred, the former are not counted in this compilation. The decline in U.S. strategic stockpiles in the 1960s mainly reflects the growing predominance of ballistic missiles over bombers. Not all published sources are in perfect agreement on these numbers. The data used here were taken from Harold Brown, "Report of Secretary of Defense to the Congress on the FY 1982 Budget, FY 1983 Authorization Request and FY 1986 Defense Programs" (1981), and Office of the Assistant Secretary of Defense, Comptroller, "National Defense Budget Estimates, FY 1983" (March 1982), among other sources.

Beyond 1983, projected increases in arsenals are shown for U.S. and S.U. arsenals as nearly vertical dashed lines, and for the sum of these arsenals as the line at the top of the figure terminating in an arrowhead. Data from Frank Barnaby, *Ambio* 11 (1982): 76–83. See also "Counterforce Issues for the U.S. Strategic Nuclear Forces," Congressional Budget Office, January 1978.

Also shown for beyond 1983 are alternative curves representing in highly schematic fashion possible reversals of the strategic arms race. For convenience, both the U.S. and the S.U. are taken as having identical arsenals after 1992. As before, the arsenals of the two nations separately, and their sum, are displayed. See text for further details.

definitely. In all natural and human systems, such steep growth rates are eventually stopped, often catastrophically.

It is widely agreed—although different people have different justifications for this conclusion—that world arsenals must be reduced significantly. There is also general agreement, with a few demurrers, that at least the early and middle stages of a significant decline can be verified by national technical means and other procedures. The first stage of major arms reduction will have to overcome a new source of reluctance, when almost all silos could be reliably destroyed in a subthreshold first strike. To overcome this reluctance, both sides will have prudently maintained an invulnerable retaliatory force, which itself would later move to subthreshold levels. (It would even be advantageous to each nation to provide certain assistance in the development of such a force by the other.) As arsenals are reduced still further, the fine tuning of the continuing decline may have to be worked very carefully and with additional safeguards to guarantee a continuing rough strategic parity. As threshold inventories are approached, some verifiable upper limits on yields as well as numbers would have to be devised to minimize the burning of cities if a nuclear conflict erupted. On the other hand, the deceleration of the arms race would have an inertia of its own, as the acceleration does; and successful first steps create a climate conducive to subsequent steps.

There are three proposals now prominently discussed in the U.S.: Nuclear Freeze, Build-down, and Deep Cuts. Their possible effects are diagrammed in figure 4. They are by no means mutually exclusive, nor do they exhaust the set of possible approaches. A negotiated Freeze would at least prevent the continuing upward escalation in stockpiles, would forestall the deployment of more destabilizing systems, and would probably be accompanied by agreement on immediate annual phased reductions (the curved lines in the middle to late 1980s in figure 4). To reduce the perceived temptation of first strike, de-MIRVing of missiles during arms reduction may be essential.

The most commonly cited method of following the Freeze

with declines in strategic inventories is incorporated in the Kennedy-Hatfield Freeze Resolution: percentage reductions. Under this approach, the two sides would agree on a percentage—often quoted as being between 5 and 10 percent—and would agree to decrease deployed warheads by that percentage annually. (The percentage would be applied to an ever lower base and, as a consequence, warhead levels would approach zero asymptotically.) The percentage reduction method was proposed to the S.U. by the U.S. at the Vienna summit in June 1979 and was to be applied to the limits and sublimits of the SALT II accords until these reached a reduction of 50 percent.

The Builddown proposal is one in which modernization is permitted, but each side must pay a price in additional reductions of warheads for each warhead mounted on a modernized missile. In many current versions of the proposal, it would also require both sides to decrease their total warhead inventories by about 5 percent a year (again, the percentage annual reduction approach) to ensure that at least some reductions would take place even if modernization did not. The rate of decline for Builddown illustrated in figure 4 is essentially that of Representative Albert Gore (1983), in which rough parity at 8,500 warheads each is adopted as a goal for 1991–92 and the levels reduced to 6,500 warheads each by 1997. There is concern that the "modernization" of strategic systems that Builddown encourages might open the door to still more destabilizing weapons. It is also by no means clear that all proponents of Build-down envision further reductions below the interim goal of about 5,000 warheads each for the U.S. and the S.U. If this rate of Build-down continued indefinitely, the world would not cross back below threshold until about the year 2020. As dramatic a change from current circumstances as this represents, in light of the present global crisis it is, I think, too leisurely a pace.

Deep Cuts, originally advocated by George Kennan (1981) and Noel Gayler (1982) as an initial halving of the global arsenals in some relatively short period of time, proposes the turning in of the fission triggers of thermonuclear weapons, deployed or undeployed, to a binational or multinational authority, and the triggers subsequently gainfully consumed in nuclear power plants (the ultimate in beating swords into plowshares). A highly schematic curve for something like Deep Cuts is also shown in figure 4, starting from Gore's assumption of parity by 1991–92. Halving of the present global arsenals would then occur around 1995, and the global arsenals would return to below the doomsday threshold by the year 2000.

The actual shape of these declining curves would very likely have kinks and wiggles in them to accommodate the details of a bilaterally—and eventually multilaterally—agreed-upon plan to reduce the arsenals without compromising the security of any of the nuclear powers. The Deep Cuts curve has a rate of decline only about as steep as the rate of rise beginning in 1970. Much steeper declines may be feasible and should be considered. It would be an act of commitment to the future, and a source of justifiable national pride, if major nuclear arms reductions were well under way by 1992 (see figure 4), which happens to be both the five hundredth anniversary of the discovery of America by Christopher Columbus, and the seventy-fifth anniversary of the Bolshevik Revolution. And reduction of the world strategic inventories to distinctly subthreshold values would be a fitting planetary goal to mark the beginning of the third millennium. To accomplish either of these objectives, significant steps must be taken immediately.

No one contends it will be easy to reverse the nuclear arms race. But it is required, at least for the same reasons that were used to justify the arms race in the first place—the national security of the U.S. and the S.U. It is necessarily an enterprise of great magnitude. John Stuart Mill said, "Against a great evil, a small remedy does not produce a small result. It produces no result at all." If the same technical ingenuity, dedication, and resources were devoted to the downward slopes in figure 4 as to the upward slopes, there is no reason to doubt that it could be negotiated safely.

In the deployment of more stabilizing weapons systems, in the possible development—especially in later stages of arms reductions—of novel means of treaty verification, and (perhaps) in the augmentation of conventional armaments, it will, of course, be expensive. But not in terms of what it would buy: in simple actuarial calculations, the value of the insurance premium is taken to depend not only on the probability of a given undesirable event occurring but also on the value of the property at risk.

To put a cash value on the world is both callous and absurd. But those are also characteristics that mark the nuclear arms race. In terms of property alone, let us take as a very crude lower limit for the value of what might be destroyed in a global thermonuclear war the Gross World Product—about $10 trillion per annum (Sivard, 1983)—times some rather hopeful recovery time, assuming that our worst fears are not realized and that 10 to 20 percent of the world population survives. A wildly optimistic value for this recovery time might be thirty years. Thus the property value of what the world has to lose in a nuclear war is substantially more than $300 trillion.

The probability of such a nuclear war happening is of course unknown, but there is a significant body of informed opinion that estimates it as highly likely in the next few decades. Again to be conservative, let us assume (for this argument only) that the average waiting time to a nuclear war is about a hundred years if we follow our present course. Under these assumptions, the fraction of the global resources we should dedicate to guaranteeing that no nuclear war ever occurs would, in a rational society, be $300 trillion times 1 percent probability per year equals $3 trillion per year, or roughly six times the planet's annual direct military expenditures.[15] If we believed, as many do, that nuclear war is more imminent, this sum would be increased proportionately.

Thus, a prudent nuclear power would spend much more

15. These have been estimated at $540 billion (Sivard, 1983).

every year to defuse the arms race and prevent nuclear war than it does on all military preparedness.[16] For comparison, in the United States the annual budget of the Department of Defense is about 10,000 times that of the Arms Control and Disarmament Agency, quite apart from any questions about the dedication and effectiveness of the ACDA. The equivalent disparity is even greater in many other nations. I believe that the technical side of guaranteeing a major multilateral and strategically secure global arms reduction can be devised and deployed for considerably less—perhaps a factor of 100 less—than $3 trillion a year.

I do not pretend these extremely crude calculations to be more than a rough guide; but they do give some feeling for the chasm that separates a prudent policy in face of our current knowledge of nuclear war from the actual present policies of the nuclear powers. Likewise, nations far removed from the conflict, even nations with little or no investment in the quarrels among the nuclear powers, stand to be destroyed in a nuclear war, rather than benefiting from the mutual annihilation of the superpowers. They also, one might think, would be wise to devote considerable resources to help ensure that nuclear war does not break out.

Summary and Conclusions

The cold, dark, radioactivity, pyrotoxins, and ultraviolet light following a nuclear war—including some scenarios involving only a small fraction of the world strategic arsenals—would imperil every survivor on the planet. There is a real danger of the extinction of humanity. A threshold exists at which the climatic catastrophe could be triggered, very roughly around 500 to 2,000 contemporary strategic warheads. A major first strike may be an act of national suicide even if no retaliation occurs. Given the magnitude of the potential loss,

16. It might be claimed that the military budgets of various nations are intended precisely for the prevention of nuclear war. If so, further increments in stockpiles and delivery systems seem to be a poor way to go about it—especially in view of the TTAPS results.

no policy declarations and no mechanical safeguards can adequately guarantee the safety of the human species. No national rivalry or ideological confrontation justifies putting the species at risk. Accordingly there is a critical need for safe and verifiable reductions of the world strategic inventories to below threshold. At such levels, still adequate for deterrence, at least the worst could not happen should a nuclear war break out.

National security policies that seem prudent or even successful during a term of office or a tour of duty may work to endanger national—and global—security over longer periods of time. In many respects it is just such short-term thinking that is responsible for the present world crisis. The looming prospect of the climatic catastrophe makes short-term thinking even more dangerous. The past has been the enemy of the present, and the present the enemy of the future. The problem cries out for an ecumenical perspective that rises above cant, doctrine, and mutual recrimination, however apparently justified, and that at least partly transcends parochial fealties in time and space. What is urgently required is a coherent, mutually agreed upon, long-term policy for dramatic reductions in nuclear armaments and a deep commitment, embracing decades, to carry it out.

Our talent, while imperfect, to foresee the future consequences of our present actions and to change our course appropriately is a hallmark of the human species and one of the chief reasons for our success over the past million years. Our future depends entirely on how quickly and how broadly we can refine this talent. We should plan for and cherish our fragile world as we do our children and our grandchildren; there will be no other place for them to live. It is nowhere ordained that we must remain in bondage to nuclear weapons.

For stimulating discussions, and/or careful reviews of an earlier version of this article, I am grateful to Hans Bethe, McGeorge Bundy, Joan Chittester, Freeman Dyson, Paul Ehrlich, Alton Frye, Richard Garwin, Noel Gayler, Jerome Grossman, Averell Harriman, Mark Harwell, John P. Holdren,

Eric Jones, George F. Kennan, Robert S. McNamara, Carson Mark, Philip Morrison, Jay Orear, William Perry, David Pimentel, Theodore Postel, George Rathjens, Joseph Rotblat, Herbert Scoville, Brent Scowcroft, John Steinbruner, Jeremy Stone, Edward Teller, Brian Toon, Richard Turco, Paul Warnke, Victor Weisskopf, Robert R. Wilson, and Albert Wohlstetter. They are, however, in no way to be held responsible for the opinions stated or the conclusions drawn. I deeply appreciate the encouragement, suggestions, and critical assessments provided by Lester Grinspoon, Steven Soter, and, especially, Ann Druyan, and the dedicated transcriptions, through many drafts, by Mary Roth.

This article would not have been possible without the high scientific competence and dedication of my coauthors on the TTAPS study (Turco et al., 1983) Richard P. Turco, Owen B. Toon, Thomas P. Ackerman, and James B. Pollack, and my nineteen coauthors of the accompanying scientific paper on the long-term biological consequences of nuclear war. Finally, I wish to thank my Soviet colleagues V. V. Alexandrov, E. I. Chazov, G. S. Golitsyn, and E. P. Velikhov, among others, for organizing independent confirmations of the probable existence of a post-nuclear war climatic catastrophe, and for helping generate a different kind of climate—one of mutual concern and cooperation that is essential if we are to emerge safely from the trap that our two nations have jointly set for ourselves, our civilization, and our species.

References

Aviation Week and Space Technology. (1979, May 15). P. 225.

Ball, D. (1981). *Adelphi paper 169.* London: International Institute for Strategic Studies.

Bergstrom, S., et al. (1983). *Effects of nuclear war on health and health services* (Publications No. A36.12). Rome: World Health Organization.

Bethe, H. A., Garwin, R. L., Gottfried, K., & Kendall, H. W. (1984). Article. *Scientific American, 251,* 39.

Bracken, P., & Shubik, M. (1982). *Technology and society* (Vol. 4).

Carter, A. B. (1984). *Directed energy missile defense in space.* Washington, DC: Office of Technology Assessment, U.S. Congress.

Chagas, C., et al. (1984, January 23–25). *Nuclear winter: A warning* (Document 11). Vatican City: Pontifical Academy of Sciences.

Covey, C., Schneider, S. H., & Thompson, S. L. (1984). Global atmospheric effects of massive smoke injections from a nuclear war: Results from general circulation model simulations. *Nature, 308,* 21–25.

Drell, S. D., Farley, P. J., & Holloway, D. (1984). *The Reagan strategic defense initiative*. Stanford, CA: International Strategic Institute, Stanford University.

Ehrlich, P. R., Harwell, M. A., Raven, P. H., Sagan, C., & Woodwell, G. M. (1983). The long-term biological consequences of nuclear war. *Science, 222,* 1293–1300.

Garwin, R. (1983, November 10). *Comments on strategic defense.* Testimony to the Subcommittee on International Security and Scientific Affairs of the Committee on Foreign Affairs, House of Representatives, U.S. Cong.

Gayler, N. (1982, April 25). How to break the momentum of the nuclear arms race. *The New York Times Magazine.*

Glasstone, S., & Dolan, P. J. (1977). *The effects of nuclear war* (3rd ed.). Washington, DC: U.S. Department of Defense.

Gore, A. (1983, August 4). *Congressional Record, 123* (114).

Hare, F. K., et al. (1985). *Nuclear winter and associated effects.* Ottawa: Royal Society of Canada.

Kennan, G. F. (1981, May 31). The only way out of the nuclear nightmare. *Manchester Guardian Weekly.*

Kruger, C. H., Setlow, R. B., et al. (1982). *Causes and effects of stratospheric ozone reduction: An update.* Washington, DC: National Academy of Sciences.

National Academy of Sciences/National Research Council. (1975). *Long-term worldwide effects of multiple nuclear weapons detonations.* Washington, DC: National Academy of Sciences.

National Research Council. (1985). *The effects on the atmosphere of a major nuclear exchange.* Washington, DC: National Academy Press.

Office of Technology Assessment, U.S. Congress. (1979). *The effects of nuclear war.* Washington, DC: U.S. Government Printing Office.

Peterson, J. (Ed.). (1982). Nuclear war: The aftermath. *Ambio* [Royal Swedish Academy of Sciences], *11*(2–3).

Pimentel, D., & Sorrells, M. (1983). Private communication.

Pittock, A. B., et al. (in press). *Environmental consequences of nuclear war: Vol. 1. Physical and atmospheric effects* (SCOPE 28). New York: John Wiley.

Sagan, C. (1985). Nuclear winter: A report from the world scientific community. *Environment, 27*(8), 12–15, 38–39.

Sivard, R. L. (1983). *World military and social expenditures.* Leesburg, VA: World Priorities.

Tirman, J. (Ed.). (1984). *The fallacy of star wars.* New York: Random House.

Turco, R. P., Toon, O. B., Ackerman, T. P., Pollack, J. B., & Sagan, C. (TTAPS). (1983). Nuclear winter: Global consequences of multiple nuclear explosions. *Science, 222,* 1283–1292.

Evolutionary and Developmental Considerations

ERIK H. ERIKSON

The potential of cosmic and specieswide destruction of nuclear winter has been described with devastating clarity in Carl Sagan's chapter. At the same time it is made clear that such an outcome has been made possible by mankind's own ingenious means of technological invention. Lester Grinspoon as editor urged us to react to all of this with "a thoughtful, not a panicky fear." He urges the psychiatric world to confront this unparalleled threat, for, he claims, "psychiatric experience makes us acutely aware of both the human potential for irrational and self-destructive acts and also the enormous human capacity for altruism, adaptation, and creative solutions to the most difficult problems." Having been challenged in this spirit to outline some "developmental aspects" of our dilemma as individuals, I must ask, what *historical maladaptations* can we recognize in it all, and where can we possibly begin to trace some potential for peace which could be promoted by a devoted and concentrated interdisciplinary as well as international effort?

This, however, calls my attention to the most inclusive frame of discussion, namely that of the status of human evolution. I have tried on a number of occasions to clarify and to find a proper name for a phenomenon that seems to me to be decisive in human development, both individual and collective. I have referred to it as "pseudospeciation," and this now seems to have attracted some attention in discussions on the future of mankind. The term refers to the fact that mankind, while one species, has divided itself throughout history—territorially, culturally, politically—into various groupings that permit their members at decisive times to consider themselves, more or less consciously and explicitly, to be the

This chapter first appeared with the title "Reflections on Ethos and War" in *The Yale Review*, 73,(4), (Summer 1984) © Yale University.

only truly human species and all others (and especially *some* others) to be less than human. This tendency has, of course, special meaning in this age of the nuclear winter, because mankind has now developed technologically to a point where one powerful pseudospecies may conclude that it can save itself from what it considers to be the malicious intentions of another, equally powerful one only by risking the total annihilation of the whole species.

In 1965 I had the opportunity to present the concept of pseudospeciation at a meeting of the Royal Society in London. The discussion on that occasion was concerned with the various roles played by ritualization in the evolution of the human species, both in daily customs and in grand rituals. As one of the few representatives of developmental psychology in a hall filled with "natural" scientists, I took it to be my task to note that mankind from the very beginning has appeared on the world scene split into tribes and nations, castes and classes, religions and ideologies, each of which acts as if it were a separate species created or planned at the beginning of "time" by supernatural will. Thus each claims not only a more or less firm sense of unique collective identity but even a kind of historical immortality. Some of these pseudospecies, indeed, have mythologized for themselves a place and a moment in the very center of the universe, where and when an especially provident deity caused it to be created superior to, or at least unique among, all others. One could go far back into prehistory and envisage mankind, for all its emerging self-consciousness, as the most naked and (except for its unique uprightness) the least identifiable animal by natural markings. But it could adorn itself flamboyantly with feathers, pelts, and paints and elevate its own kind into a mythological species, often, in fact, called by whatever name it had for "the people."

Julian Huxley and Konrad Lorenz seemed to take an interest in this, and it was the latter who first used the term "pseudospeciation" *(Scheingattung)*. In this volume, we can count on an even more up-to-date evolutionist statement by Stephen Jay Gould on humanity's "genetic integrity."

At its friendliest, "pseudo" means only that something has come to appear to be what it is not; and, indeed, in the name of its pseudospecies mankind could endow itself and its universe with tools and weapons, roles and rules, legends and myths and rituals, all of which would bind a collective together and give to its existence the kind of superindividual significance that inspires not only hard work and sacrifice but also a very special loyalty, as well as heroism, fellowship—and poetry. Some peoples and cultures have peacefully cultivated just such an existence for long periods of time. What renders this "natural" process a potential malignancy of universal dimensions, however, is the fact that in times of threat and upheaval the idea of being the foremost species tends to be reinforced by a fanatic fear and hatred of other pseudospecies. The feelings that those others must be annihilated or kept "in their places" by warfare or conquest or the force of harsh custom can become a periodical and reciprocal obsession of mankind.

At its unfriendliest, then, "pseudo" means that some people are trying with all the semisincerity of propaganda to put something over on themselves as well as on others. This particular aspect of man's collective identities can become dominant under the impact of historical and economic displacements, which make a group's idealized sense of itself both more defensive and more exclusive. Such a process has become and remained so fundamental to man that, as modern history shows repeatedly, the pseudospecies mentality refuses to yield even to vast human gains in knowledge and experience. Even the most "advanced" nations can harbor—and, in fact, make fanatically explicit—a mystical adherence to the mentality of pseudospeciation. The total victory of that mentality in its most rabid form in an enlightened modern nation is exemplified, of course, in Hitler's Germany.

And yet history also provides a way by which the pseudospecies mentality of warring groups can be shared, diffused, and, as it were, become nonviolent, within the evolution of a wider identity. This can come about as the result of territorial unification: the Pax Romana, for example, embraced a remarkable variety of territories and national units. Technological advances in universal traffic, too, have the capacity to unite: from seafaring to wireless communication, they have spread changes eventually contained in a widening sense of identity which helps overcome *some* territorial and economic fear, some anxiety of cultural change, and the dread of a spiritual vacuum. History, then, has its (necessarily contradictory) ways of pseudospeciation, and we must learn to recognize similar trends in all superidentities, including our own, and especially also those that seem to be endangering our own. Thus we must learn at this time to review the modern history of the most threatening ideological and nuclear counterpart, and recognize within the Russian Revolution, for example (in its historical and geographical relativities), the development toward a more inclusive identity that eventually may yet contribute to a more universal peace.

To such a basic human phenomenon a professional worker can contribute only such insights as he can grasp with the concepts at his disposal, in the state of his field and even the story of his own life, and all that at his moment in history. In my case, it was the concept of "identity crisis," which became in some circles an almost too personal slogan and first had to be recognized as a normative stage in individual and historical human development. I. myself might not have thought of that term, however, or have been listened to so widely, if I had not come to this country. For by its very history and nature, America is the most extensive attempt to create a new national identity out of the identities of refugees and immigrants coming from virtually all the races and cultures of the world.

As one of those immigrants, I can only savor the fact that Lincoln, with his passionate restraint, named his own people "the almost chosen people." For a new kind of potentially all-human self-image took over in America, that of *the self-made man,* with a new and flexible tradition created by self-chosen immigrants on a vast and "empty" continent ready for joint improvisation. This self-image, of course, for a while left out the Indians, who had been at home in that "emptiness," and the blacks, whose immigration was anything but self-chosen. Such cruel oversight, as we now know, has usually been an ugly, if implicit, part of any new "way of life."

But in order to understand the possibilities of a wider identity, it is important to recognize the developmental necessity of at least some speciation in the communal morality of every individual. It is here that the psychiatric as well as the normative observation of life histories must teach us what is universally human. For mankind is, in Ernst Mayr's terms, the "generalist" animal, with the capacity to be born into, to adapt to, and to learn to shape the most varied environments, from the Arctic to the steaming jungle to New York City. To perform such feats evolution has provided us with a long childhood characterized by a basic minimum of instinctive patterning and a maximum of (in Freud's term) free instinctual energy available for investment in the adaptation to a vast variety of basic psychosocial patterns. But this also calls (as Freud recognized) for the development of an individual conscience, which is only a version of a communal one and thus partakes in a speciation characterized by the ritualizations typical of "our kind." And, in principle, a good communal conscience is necessary for the establishment of that widened sense of "I" which is the center of clear human awareness; while a "bad," overstrict conscience enforced by what Freud called the superego can become all too "super" and weigh the "I" as well as the ego down. Thus, human consciousness is always also burdened with negative identities—that is, all that one must not appear to be (and yet deep down feels one is); as, indeed, it has been weighed down by name-calling in earliest childhood which, in fact, is often associated with the names of detested "species"—"you pig!" "you snake!" "you rat!" Name-calling, in fact, is an important function of what Joan Erikson and I have called the "antipathic" traits that emerge beside the "sympathetic" ones in each stage of life: thus, in adulthood, beside a central generativity expressed in productivity and creativity as well as in procreativity, there is also a specific rejectivity directed against everybody that one does not care to *be like* or, indeed, like to *care for* (see E. H. Erikson, *The Life Cycle Completed: A Review* [New York: Norton, 1982]).

Developmental thinking can thus help us understand the various ways in which cultural and national units have lived and fought for positive identities—in some ways totally exclusive of each other and yet also potentially complementary to one another. On a number of occasions over the years I have even yielded to the temptation to redefine the Golden Rule in terms of a developmental ethos vitalizing a way of life guided by an increasingly informed faith rather than merely a righteous formula of conduct. "An adult," so this rule proclaims, "should strive to do to another what will enhance the other's development (at his age, in his condition, and under his circumstances) while at the same time enhancing his, the doer's, own development—at his age, in his condition, and under his circumstances." For this, of course, we have to want to learn to know a lot about others as well as ourselves: but such awareness today is well within our grasp. And I think there is every reason to assume that groups living in the same period of history, even if at different stages of collective development, can learn to evolve analogous "golden" rules. Thus, the universal spread of developmental enlightenment could eventually lead to a worldwide sharing of observations made on children, for example, in every part of the world; and this, in turn, might foster a shared awareness of the specieswide similarities of human potentials everywhere.

This worldwide sharing of newly discovered laws of child development, in turn, may before long reveal the existence of another developmental potential in human evolution—that is, new styles of "caring" by both sexes. Informed adults (and this time we may especially hope women) in this "century of the child" will simply not be able to tolerate the dangers in which children of the future will be fated to live unless things change: matters of war and peace, instead of being subject to totally unpredictable accidents of fate, must become subject to long-range planning. This must work toward the creation of a new international ethos—a shared *caring* for what is growing on this earth rather than a pervasive competitive exploitation of its resources.

To this end we must even hope that the tenuous coexistence of ethics and total warfare will prove unsupportable in our time. Even the male, the more military mind (on all "sides"!), may come to fear for its historical identity when technological conditions make both heroism and victory impossible.

How can the present deadlock in international ethics be broken? So far, at least, the most courageous protests, the most incisive interpretations, the most prophetic warnings all speak of a catastrophe so all-consuming (and indeed, a nuclear winter) that most people will have no choice but to more or less ignore it, as we are apt to do with our own deaths and, over the centuries, have done with the monotonous threats of hell.

It seems evident, then, that only a new ethical orientation, a new focus for vigorous cooperation, can free today's energies from their bondage in armed defensiveness. We live at a time in which, in spite of the specieswide destruction possible—perhaps even because of it—we can conceive for the first time of a specieswide identity, of a truly universal ethos of neighborliness such as that which has been basic for all the great world religions.

Ethos, however, cannot be fabricated—nor can ethics be imposed. Under present conditions what is necessary is not only that we recognize inequality but that we learn to respect the historical uniqueness of each state and each people. Insofar as a nation thinks of itself as a collective individual, it may begin to realize its task as being that of maintaining mutuality in international relations. For the only alternative to armed competition would seem to be an effort to activate in our "neighbors" what will strengthen their historical development, even as it strengthens us in our own, toward a shared future identity.

Professionally speaking, then, this to me also suggests, at this moment of specieswide crisis, some evolving evolutionary usefulness of an international dialogue on developmental studies. For there can be little doubt that men and women of many diverse cultures are becoming more responsive to the universal nature of childhood as a binding all-human phenomenon. And as the fathers become more receptive to the experience of relating to infants, they (as well as the mothers) may learn to use man's technological genius for the development rather than the destruction of mankind. At the same time, it is to be hoped that the mothers (as well as the fathers) will be given a more universal chance to express in communal and even in political life what has been basic to evolution and has come first in every one of our lives: namely, the powerful potential of protective mothering. Only thus can humankind truly become in spirit what it already is in fact: one species.

A Biological Comment on Erikson's Notion of Pseudospeciation

STEPHEN JAY GOULD

Speciation—the splitting of biological lineages—is the fundamental process of evolutionary change. It is not, as some have maintained, an incidental process, a kind of biological luxury producing many iterated variants of a successful theme evolved by gradual transformation within a lineage. Rather, most morphological novelties arise coincidentally with the process of branching itself (and most branches, or new species, are remarkably stable after their origin and establishment). The origin of new features in evolution is critically dependent upon the production of new lineages by branching from ancestral stocks (not by the *in toto* transformation of these stocks). Branching usually occurs when small populations become spatially isolated from their parental stocks and therefore free to diverge.

The process that Erikson has labeled "pseudospeciation" has one important similarity with, and one crucial difference from, true speciation as defined within evolutionary biology. The similarity involves an identical topology of fragmentation leading to diversification. The crucial difference, well understood by Erikson in his choice of "pseudo" as a modifying prefix, contrasts potential lability with true irrevocability.

Biological speciation is not defined by morphological difference or ecological separation but rather by the attainment of irrevocable independence from ancestors. A population becomes a new species when it accumulates sufficient genetic distinction from a parental stock that the two groups no longer interbreed—the new species, in technical parlance, has achieved "reproductive isolation." With this rupture of physical and genetic contact, the new species has become a unique

This chapter first appeared in *The Yale Review,* 73(4) (summer 1984) ©
Yale University.

lineage, permanently separate from all others on the tree of
life. Species may participate in all manner of ecological contact, from severe competition to inextricable symbiosis, but
their own genetic integrity cannot be compromised. The tree
of life (an accurate metaphor for evolutionary history) shunts
lineages into divergent twigs and branches that cannot, subsequent to their separation, anastomose with any other independent twig (except for some plant species—and there are
always some exceptions in the multifarious world of life—that
can hybridize with others to produce new amalgamated species by a process of chromosomal doubling, called allopoly-
ploidy, in hybrid cells).

Pseudospeciation, on the other hand, can never be irrevocable because humans form a single genetic pool with no
physical bar to interbreeding between males and females of
the most diverse cultural and racial groups. One pseudospecies, in designating itself as *the* people, may characterize
another as degenerate, filthy, untouchable, and nonhuman,
but no matter how intense the mutual denigration, both
groups remain members of a single biological species and
therefore capable of contact and even amalgamation should
cultural traditions change. It is biologically interesting that
neither long-term and widespread geographic separation nor
intense hostility between pseudospecies in contact has ever led
to any detectable degree of reproductive isolation between
human groups. Our genetic unity is powerful; our separa-
tions, in the long perspective of evolutionary time, absolutely
trivial.

This biological distinction between speciation and pseudospeciation leads to my second evolutionist's comment upon
Erikson's statement. He hopes that, for our survival in a nuclear age, this old and powerful tendency to pseudospeciation can be overcome either by amalgamation or by simple
mutual respect for differences, if only inspired by a recognition of the selfish benefits thus acquired. One might therefore (indeed, at least in the pop literature of science writing,
one often does) ask an evolutionary biologist: is this reversal
of our old tendency to fragmentation and warfare biologi-

cally possible? Are we not genetically programmed to be violent and territorial, an unfortunate heritage of descent from a killer ape (a notion popularized by Robert Ardrey but having no scientific support, since our australopithecine forebears were probably more vegetarian than carnivorous)?

Although much of pop human sociobiology presents facile and pessimistic scenarios holding, ipso facto, that everything commonly done by humans must be directly programmed and at least originally adaptive, I join Erikson in his cautious optimism. I find no genetic or biological barrier to a potential elimination of our tendency to pseudospeciate by identifying our own group as the chosen people and others as beyond the pale of humanity. I say this for two reasons.

The first, mentioned by Erikson, lies in our biological status—a result of our egregiously large brains—as maximal "generalists" with "a basic minimum of instinctive patterning and a maximum of free instinctual energy available for investment in a variety of basic pseudosocial encounters." It is our biology that makes us free, not our social hopes for a better world. The solution to the false dichotomy of nature and nurture lies here: the flexibility that gives nurture such power (and that might allow us to overcome the age-old but nonprogrammed cultural habits of pseudospeciation) arises directly from our *biological* status as large-brained, neotenic primates.

The second reason, an important biological fact unfortunately unknown to most people, inheres in the remarkably small genetic distinctions among human racial groups. We are truly one biological species with trivial differences among our groups. Again, this statement is not the mushy claim of liberal sentimentality but a contingent fact of history. It might well have been otherwise. Our apish australopithecine ancestors might have survived and confronted us with the existence of a truly inferior but partly human species. Or racial differentiation within *Homo sapiens* might have occurred very long ago, permitting enough time for significant genetic differences to accumulate between groups. Human history could have unfolded in such a way and confronted us with different moral dilemmas, but it didn't.

Human races are different in a few highly visible characters (like skin color and hair form). This leads many people to a seat-of-the-pants feeling that racial differences must be substantial. Genetic techniques for assessing overall similarity have become available only since the mid-1960s, and their single clear and outstanding result is the astonishingly small amount of genetic variation among races. We are a highly variable species, but almost all genetic differentiation occurs among members of local populations, not between races—that is, each race is highly variable, but the spectrum of variation differs little among groups. As my colleague Richard Lewontin, who did much of the original work on overall genetic distances among human races, states with graphic emphasis: if (God forbid) the holocaust comes and all humans are killed except for one tiny tribe in the New Guinea highlands, we will have lost little of the genetic diversity within *Homo sapiens*.

The surprising triviality of genetic differentiation among human racial groups can mean only that racial separation within *Homo sapiens* is, again in the perspective of evolutionary time, a very recent phenomenon, probably no more than tens of thousands of years—a geological microsecond. Whatever the historical and psychological depth of our tendency to pseudospeciate, it is not based on genetic differences among human groups. We find, therefore, no biological impediment to the elimination of this lamentable tendency.

Imagining the Real:
Beyond the Nuclear "End"

ROBERT JAY LIFTON

The first promise of the atomic age is that it can make some of our nightmares come true. The capacity painfully acquired by normal men to distinguish between sleep, delusion, hallucination, and the objective reality of waking life has for the first time in human history been seriously weakened.

EDWARD GLOVER
War, Sadism, and Pacifism, p. 274

The appearance of nuclear weapons in the mid-1940s, symbolized by the visual image of an over-whelming mushroom cloud, evoked a broader conceptual image: that of man's extermination of his species by means of his own technology. The image, of course, is not totally new. Versions of it have been constituted by visionaries—H. G. Wells is an outstanding example—at least from the time of the Industrial Revolution. The concept of nuclear winter gives concrete substance to that image: using just a small portion of our nuclear stockpiles, we may so impair our habitat, the earth, that it no longer can sustain human and other forms of life. Never has the human imagination been called upon to encompass an image quite like that.

The element of self-extermination must be differentiated from older religious images of Armageddon, Final Judgment, or the end of the world. Terrifying as these may be, they are part of a cosmology that envisions the apocalyptic conclusion to human history as a redemptive event. Man is acted upon by a higher power who destroys only for spiritual purposes, such as achieving the kingdom of God. That is a far cry from man's destruction of himself with his own tools and to no discernible purpose.

Several special features mark this contemporary end-of-the-world imagery. There is first the suggestion of something on the order of biological extinction. Second, the image is related to specific external events of recent history—Hiroshima and Nagasaki as well as the Nazi death camps. And third, unlike earlier imagery of world destruction—even that associated with such events as the plagues of the Middle Ages—the danger comes from the designs and imperatives of human technology. Our "end" is in considerable measure perceived as a form of self-destruction. We therefore see in it little justification, only absurdity. If some view nuclear ho-

locaust as inevitable, they do so with resignation or hopeless-
ness as opposed to the meaningful inevitability of an eschatology or submission to irresistible forces of nature.

This potential self-destruction has bearing on issues of
widespread guilt as well as on psychic numbing, our diminished capacity to feel. We are compelled to imagine ourselves as both executioner and victim, the two roles Camus
warned us never to assume. We numb ourselves both toward
destruction itself and toward our guilt as potential perpetra-
tors of that destruction. Traditionally, guilt is contained within
an eschatology: if man is guilty, he must be punished, he must
be destroyed in order to be re-created in purer form. Within
our present context, however, one perceives the threat of a
literal, absolute end without benefit of a belief system that
gives form to that idea or solace to those who hold it.

Given the temptation of despair, our need can be simply
stated: We must confront the image that haunts us, making
use of whatever models we can locate. Only then can we
achieve those changes in consciousness that must accompany
(if not precede) changes in public policy on behalf of a human future. We must look into the abyss in order to be able
to see beyond it.

Calling forth a mental picture of the end of the world,
however, is a demanding imaginative·task and itself has many
pitfalls. Much depends upon context. If we are to move
toward the kind of imagination we require, we need first to
look, sometimes in odd places, at examples of end-of-the-world
imagery. In this chapter I will examine that imagery as it occurred in Hiroshima and as it occurs in schizophrenia, which
turns out to have relevance for us beyond the pathological.
Then I will suggest a psychological model or paradigm that
enables us to approach and evaluate the imagery in these situations as well as in millennial religious movements. We will
then be in a position to take a new look at the current nuclear threat. I will try to show how the concept of nuclear
winter enhances our imaginative task, sharpens our understanding of the dangerous contemporary ideology I call "nuclearism," and thereby contributes to the quest for life-en-
hancing alternatives.

A logical place to start is Hiroshima—not because it is in any way equivalent to the destruction of a nuclear winter but rather because it provides a beginning model for the imagination.

Hiroshima and the End of the World

When the atomic bomb was dropped over Hiroshima, the most striking psychological feature of survivors' response was the immediate and absolute shift from normal existence to an overwhelming encounter with death. A shopkeeper's assistant conveys this feeling characteristically, without explicit end-of-the-world imagery but in a tone consistent with that imagery:

> It came very suddenly. . . . I felt something like an electric short—a bluish sparkling light. . . . There was a noise, and I felt great heat—even inside the house. . . . I didn't know anything about the atomic bomb so I thought that some bomb had fallen directly upon me. . . . And then when I felt that our house had been directly hit, I became furious. . . . There were roof tiles and walls—everything black—entirely covering me. So I screamed for help. . . . And from all around I heard moans and screaming, and then I felt a kind of danger to myself. . . . I thought that I too was going to die in that way. I felt this way at that moment because I was absolutely unable to do anything at all by my own power. . . . I didn't know where I was or what I was under. . . . I couldn't hear voices of my family. I didn't know how I could be rescued. I felt I was going to suffocate and then die, without knowing exactly what happened to me. This was the kind of expectation I had. (Lifton, 1984, p. 21)

Survivors recalled initial feelings related to death and dying, such as "This is the end for me," or "My first feeling was 'I think I will die.' " But beyond those feelings was the sense that *the whole world was dying.* That sense was expressed by a physicist who was covered with debris and temporarily blinded:

> My body seemed black, everything seemed dark, dark all over. . . . Then I thought, "The world is ending." (p. 22)

A Protestant minister, himself uninjured, but responding to the mutilation and destruction he saw everywhere around him, experienced his end-of-the-world imagery in an apocalyptic Christian idiom:

> The feeling I had was that everyone was dead. The whole city was destroyed. . . . I had thought all of my family must be dead—it doesn't matter if I die. . . . I thought this was the end of Hiroshima—of Japan—of humankind. . . . This was God's judgment on man. (p. 22)

His memory is inseparable from his theology, just as everyone's memory of such events is inseparable from his or her fundamental interpretive principles.

A woman writer also recalled religious imagery, probably Buddhist:

> I just could not understand why our surroundings had changed so greatly in one instant. . . . I thought it might have been something which had nothing to do with the war, the collapse of the earth which it was said would take place at the end of the world, and which I had read about as a child. (Ota, 1955, p. 63)

This sense of world collapse could also be expressed symbolically, as in the immediate thought of a devoutly religious domestic worker: "There is no God, no Buddha" (Lifton, 1984, p. 23).

Some responded with humor, inevitably gallows humor, as a way of mocking their own helplessness and the absurdity of total destruction. A professional cremator, for instance, though severely burned, managed to make his way back to his home (adjoining the crematorium) and felt relieved because "I thought I would die soon, and it would be convenient to have the crematorium close by" (Lifton, 1984, p. 23).

Many recollections convey the dreamlike grotesqueness of the scene of the dead and the dying, and the numbed wandering of the living. This is sensitively rendered by Dr. Michihiko Hachiya in his classic *Hiroshima Diary:*

> Those who were able walked silently toward the suburbs in the distant hills, their spirits broken, their initiative gone. When asked whence they had come, they pointed to the city and said "that way": and when asked where they were going, pointed away from the city and said "this way." They were so broken and confused that they moved and behaved like automatons.
>
> Their reactions had astonished outsiders who reported with amazement the spectacle of long files of people holding stolidly to a narrow, rough path when close by was a smooth easy road going in the same direction. The outsiders could not grasp the fact that they were witnessing the exodus of a people who walked in the realm of dreams. (Hachiya, 1955, pp. 54–55)

People characterized those they saw in such strange states (near-naked, bleeding, faces disfigured and bloated from burns, arms held awkwardly away from the body to prevent friction with other burned areas), and by implication themselves, as being "like so many beggars" or "like . . . red Jizo standing on the sides of the road" (Jizo: a Buddhist deity whose images in natural stone can be found along roads and paths). Above all, there was so great a sense of silence as to suggest the absence of all life. Again the woman writer:

> It was quiet around us. . . . in fact there was a fearful silence which made one feel that all people and all trees and vegetation were dead. (Ota, 1955, p. 3)

Similarly, Dr. Hachiya was struck by the "uncanny stillness" permeating his hospital:

> One thing was common to everyone I saw—complete silence . . . why was everyone so quiet? . . . it was as though I walked through a gloomy, silent motion picture. (Hachiya, 1955, pp. 4, 5, 37)

In all this there was a profound disruption in the relationship between death and life. This confusion of distinction between one's sense of being alive or dead was conveyed by a grocer, himself severely burned:

> The appearance of people was . . . well, they all had
> skin blackened by burns. . . . They had no hair because
> their hair was burned, and at a glance you couldn't tell
> whether you were looking at them from in front or in
> back. . . . They held their arms bent [forward] like this
> [he proceeded to demonstrate their position] . . . and
> their skin—not only on their hands, but on their faces
> and bodies too—hung down. . . . If there had been only
> one or two such people . . . perhaps I would not have
> had such a strong impression. But wherever I walked I
> met these people. . . . Many of them died along the
> road—I can still picture them in my mind—like walking
> ghosts. . . . They didn't look like people of this world.
> . . . They had a special way of walking—very slowly.
> . . . I myself was one of them. (Lifton, 1984, p. 27)

Whatever life remained seemed unrelated to a natural order and more part of a supernatural or unnatural one. These impressions emerged in frequently expressed imagery of a Buddhist hell that seemed to provide an interpretation for understanding the immediate situation. A young sociologist's description:

> My immediate thought was that this was like the hell I
> had always read about. . . . I had never seen anything
> which resembled it before, but I thought that should
> there be a hell, this was it—the Buddhist hell, where we
> were taught that people who could not attain salvation
> always went. . . . And I imagined that all of these peo-
> ple who could not attain salvation always went. . . . And
> I imagined that all of these people I was seeing were in
> the hell that I had read about. (Lifton, 1984, p. 29)

These Hiroshima memories, then, combine explicit end-of-the-world imagery with a grotesque dreamlike aura of a nonnatural situation, a form of existence in which life is so permeated by death as to become virtually indistinguishable from it.

Schizophrenia and the End of the World

Daniel Paul Schreber, a distinguished German judge, could hardly have realized when he published his *Memoirs of My Nervous Illness* in 1903, that he was providing psychoanalytic psychiatry with a landmark "case." From these memoirs Freud constructed a concept of schizophrenia, especially paranoid schizophrenia, that has informed, haunted, and confused psychiatric work on psychosis ever since.

Schreber was preoccupied with the idea of a "world catastrophe," which at times he thought was necessary for the re-creation of the species. In one passage he describes some of this delusional system in connection with observations on the stars and mysterious cosmic events:

> When later I regularly visited the garden and again saw—my memory does not fully deceive me—two suns in the sky at the same time, one of which was our earthly sun. The other was said to be the Cassiopeian group of stars drawn together into a single sun. From the sum total of my recollections, my impression gained hold of me that the period in question, which according to human calculations stretched over three to four months, had covered an immensely long period. It was as if single nights had a duration of centuries. So that within that time the most profound alterations in the whole of mankind, and the earth itself, and the whole solar system might very well have taken place. It was repeatedly mentioned in visions that the work of the past 1400 years had been lost. (Schreber, 1955, pp. 84–85)

When Schreber says "repeatedly mentioned" he refers to his "visions" or hallucinations. He interprets the figure of 1,400 years to be an indication of "the duration of time that the earth has been populated" and remembers hearing another figure, about 200 or 212 years, for the time still "allotted to the earth."

> During the latter part of my stay in Flechsig's Asylum [Prof. Flechsig was the director] I thought this period had already expired and therefore I was the last real human being left, and that the few human shapes I saw apart from myself—Professor Flechsig, some attendants, occasional more or less strange-looking patients—were only "fleeting improvised men" created by miracle. I pondered over such possibilities as that the whole of Flechsig's Asylum or perhaps the city of Leipzig with it had been "dug out" and moved to some other celestial body, all of them possibilities which questions asked by the voices who talked to me seemed to hint at, as for instance whether Leipzig was still standing, etc. I regarded the starry sky largely, if not wholly, extinguished.

Here the world catastrophe is accompanied by re-creation, with Schreber himself at the center of it. Thus he goes on to speak of seeing "beyond the walls of the Asylum only a narrow strip of land," so strange and different that "at times one spoke of a holy landscape."

> I lived for years in doubt as to whether I was really still on earth or whether on some other celestial body. . . .
> In the soul-language during [that] time . . . I was called *"the seer of spirits,"* that is, a man who sees, and is in communication with, spirits or departed souls. (pp. 85–88)

These quotations from Schreber convey the kind of end-of-the-world imagery one encounters in acute and chronic forms of psychosis, usually paranoid schizophrenic psychosis. The psychotic dies *with* the world in that his sense of inner disintegration includes self and world. But by rendering himself at the same time the only survivor, he expresses the paranoid struggle with power and vitality and a distorted paranoid vision of regeneration. These schizophrenic end-of-the-world images would seem to be in sharp contrast with those experienced in Hiroshima: the one an expression of delusion and inner disorder, the other of actuality and externally imposed destruction. But the distinction is far from absolute. In Hiroshima, for instance, the overwhelming *external* event stimulates an immediate and corresponding internal experience, something like internal breakdown or overwhelming psychological trauma. And although we usually think of schizophrenia as a strictly *internal* derangement, it too is subject to external influences and to the struggle for some kind of meaning structure. Hence the content, style, and impact of the condition upon others—the dialogue or nondialogue between schizophrenic people and society—all this varies enormously with historical time and place. Correspondingly, the end-of-the-world imagery of schizophrenia is strongly affected by historical and technological context. We may say that the external threat of contemporary nuclear weapons approaches the terrain of schizophrenia.

More generally, end-of-the-world imagery is a fundamental imaginative capacity at the far reaches of the human mind, a capacity we must now call upon if we are, in Martin Buber's phrase, to "imagine the real."

Death and the Continuity of Life—Proximate and Ultimate Levels

To claim, as I have, that schizophrenia has relevance for all end-of-the-world imagery requires the use of a psychological model or paradigm that I would like to outline briefly here. The same paradigm enables us to find common ground among the various end-of-the-world images I discuss in this essay.

The paradigm presumes both a proximate or immediate level of experience and an ultimate level close to what Tillich called "ultimate concern." That is, the schizophrenic not only fears annihilation but, as Searles and others point out, fears (and to some extent welcomes) his being severed from the great stream of human existence. There can be an element of ecstasy in the schizophrenic perception of the end of the world, along with terror. Indeed, this very fear of being historically annihilated is a matter that needs much additional psychological attention.

Our paradigm, then, is that of death and the continuity of life—or, one may say, the symbolization of life and death. The proximate level involves the immediate nitty-gritty experiences dealt with in most psychological work. The ultimate dimension involves connections beyond the self, reflecting our biological and historical connectedness, or what I call the symbolization of immortality. Involved in the struggle for symbolic immortality is the struggle for connection with those who have gone before and those who will follow our own limited life span.

This sense of immortality is sought normatively, through living on in one's children, one's works, one's human influences, and in something we look on as eternal nature. Continuity is also experienced in religious belief or spiritual principle, whether or not it literally postulates a life after death, and, finally, in any direct experience of transcendence, in psychic states so intense that time and death disappear. This last case is the classic mode of the mystics and is not unrelated to various experiences of end-of-the-world imagery. Such experiential transcendence can be spiritual; it may be sexual; it can occur through athletics or the contemplation of beauty. It is sometimes spoken of as "Dionysian," but it can take quiet forms as well.

Concern with connections beyond the self, what I call the ultimate dimension, is often left solely to the theologians and the philosophers. This is a mistake that I feel those of us involved in psychological work should redress. What is involved here is an evolutionary triad. To become human one takes on simultaneously: first, the knowledge that one will die; second, the symbolizing function, which I take to be the fundamental form of human mentation, requiring the internal re-creation of all that we perceive; and third, the creation of culture, which is by no means merely a vehicle for denying death (as many psychoanalytic thinkers, from Freud to Norman O. Brown, have claimed) but is integral to man the cultural animal and probably necessary for the development of the kind of brain he has come to possess.

When the image of nuclear winter threatens our symbolization of immortality, then, it threatens a level of psychic experience that defines our humanity.

The immediate or proximate level of experience involves
three dialectics—connection versus separation, movement
versus stasis, and integrity versus disintegration. The negative end of the dialectic is what I call the death equivalent.
Each of the three is familiar, having its beginning or prefi-
guring in various inchoate experiences from birth and perhaps before. The sequence is from the physiological (in terms
of connection-separation, the newborn seeking out the breast,
and later the mother) to the creation of images (the infant
forming pictures of its mother and recognizing her) to symbolization (the eventual capacity for complex feelings of love,
loyalty connections). Similarly, the newborn may cry when
physically "separated" from its mother, and the developing
infant, from early images of separation and loss, constructs
a psychological substrate for the slightly later exposure to the
idea of death. Thus, over the course of the life cycle, immediate involvements of connection and separation, movement
and stasis, and integrity and disintegration become highly
symbolized into elaborate ethical and psychological constel-
lations.

When the image of nuclear winter threatens this proximate level of experience, it undermines and instills fear and
doubt in our sense of moving safely through ordinary steps
in the life cycle.

Nuclear Threat: Fear and Futurelessness

For the individual person, nuclear threat does not in itself
cause any particular symptom, action, or pattern of behavior. At the same time, nothing in our existence—certainly
nothing that we plan or contemplate over time—is entirely
free of its imagery of extinction. That imagery is associated
with fear and futurelessness.

What we call nuclear fear, then, includes fear of death, our
own and that of family members and others close to us; fear
of bodily assaults, including severe burns and keloids; and

the special terror of "invisible contamination"—the unending danger of delayed radiation effects—that haunted Hiroshima survivors. Nuclear fear is intensified by a quality of the
unknown—by the amorphousness, mystery, and totality of
impact we associate with the weapons. Nuclear fear does not
occur in isolation but interacts with the rest of life's more ordinary struggles. A growing body of research demonstrates
that children and adolescents experience various kinds of fear,
powerlessness, and rage and that they feel abandoned and
unprotected in a situation increasingly out of human control
(Mack, 1983). These fears make important contact with the
feelings of separation, stasis, and disintegration that we have
identified as death equivalents.

Nuclear futurelessness has to do with a radical interrup-
tion in our sense of being part of the Great Chain of Being,
in our sense of larger human connectiveness or symbolic immortality. We do not cease to attempt to live on in our children and impact on others, abandon our spiritual attain-
ments, or renounce our ties to nature and the search for "high
"states"of transcendence; rather, we have doubts about all these
modes, about anything being able to persist. Again there is
special significance in what we have learned from children of
the nuclear age. We know that they go about playing, studying, preparing for work and marriage, and doing all the other
things that they associate with adulthood. But at the same time
they experience the sense that this may be a sham, that they
are preparing for nothing, that there will be little or no adult
existence. From the children we learn about our own double
life, our own doubts about a human future.

At the same time we respond as adults with special inten-
sity to the suffering and courage of children: to Anne Frank's
expressions of love and hope prior to being murdered by the
Nazis, and to a similar figure in Hiroshima, Sadako Sasaki,
who was exposed to the bomb at the age of two and was a
healthy, vigorous child until stricken with leukemia ten years
later. She struggled to sustain her life by folding paper cranes,
in keeping with a Japanese folk belief that since the crane
lives a thousand years the folding of a thousand paper cranes

cures one of illness. The monument to Sadako is perhaps the
most popular structure in Hiroshima's Peace Park, always
covered with paper cranes and surrounded by children.
  In Japan Sadako's story has been told and retold in books
and film and has come to symbolize the bomb's desecration
of the pure and vulnerable—of childhood itself. We respond
to that desecration because we love and feel responsible for
our children, because we judge ourselves by what we subject
them to, and because they symbolize for us more than anything else the larger human future. The children are ourselves.

Nuclear Winter: A Contribution to the Imagination

  Nuclear winter serves us well in these imaginative struggles, because in making concrete the idea of the nuclear end
it clarifies our existential situation and helps us liberate ourselves from illusion. Nuclear winter tells us, loud and clear,
precisely where hope lies: not in shelters, evacuation plans,
and "rebuilding" from the ruins but *only* in prevention. In
that way we are helped as psychological professionals in carrying out our task of exposing as illusions any concepts of
preparing for nuclear holocaust, protecting ourselves and
others, recovering from its effects.
  Nuclear winter also prods our imaginations in the direction of nothingness—a direction we must explore to grasp our
predicament. Here, a brief return to Hiroshima is useful.
  A history professor I interviewed in Hiroshima told me of
witnessing the bomb's destruction from the outskirts of the
city:

> I climbed Hijiyama Hill and looked down. I saw that Hi-
> roshima had disappeared. . . . I was shocked by the
> sight. . . . what I felt then and still feel now I just can't
> explain with words. . . . Hiroshima didn't exist. That
> was mainly what I saw. Hiroshima just didn't exist.

When asked how he thought Hiroshima should be commem-
orated, he said that there should be a wide area around the

hypocenter in which there was absolutely *nothing,* and that on August 6, the commemoration day, no one should stir, all homes and stores should be closed. Hiroshima would then become "a city of the dead," and people would learn the simple truth that "the atomic weapon converts everything into nothing."

When I visited Auschwitz recently, in connection with research on Nazi doctors, I saw many exhibits there that spared little in revealing what human beings can do to other human beings. But the two exhibits that had the strongest impact on me were one that was simply a room full of shoes, many of them baby shoes; and another, a room full of suitcases of the old-fashioned rectangular kind with the addresses of people on them. Such exhibits require the viewer to do the psychological work of imagining the missing people. It is their absence—the element of nothingness—that captures the imagination.

But the threat of extinction and nothingness can provoke problematic responses as well, millennial imagery called forth clinically or theologically in the name of regeneration. In schizophrenia and other clinical syndromes, Freud understood symptoms to express attempts at what he called "restitution" of the disordered self to a healthier state. That principle has particular relevance to imagery of the end of the world, and in the Schreber case we saw how that imagery was bound up with the idea of the world as being purified and reconstituted. In millennial imagery associated with religious thought, the element of revitalization and moral cleansing—the vision of a new and better existence—is even more prominent and considerably more functional. Theological tradition can provide form, coherence, and shared spiritual experience in contrast to the isolated delusional system of the individual schizophrenic person.

Ultimately we may say that millennial ideas of all kinds are associated with an even larger category of mythological imagery of death and rebirth. They represent later theological invocations and refinements of that earlier fundamental category. We miss the significance of millennial imagery if we see in it *only* the threat of deadness or the absence of meaning; but we also misunderstand it if we do not recognize in it precisely that threat and absence. In other words, millennial imagery includes something on the order of death equivalents—of threatened annihilation—and at the same time, in its various symbolizations, something on the order of renewal and revitalization.

In schizophrenia that imagery of revitalization is radically literalized. With desymbolization there is an inability to carry out the specific human task of constant creation and re-creation of images and forms, or what I call the formative-symbolizing function. Schizophrenia involves a fundamental impairment to this function, the replacement of symbolic flow with static literalization.

An important question for religious millennial imagery is the extent to which it is experienced in literalized, as opposed to more formative or symbolized, ways. Toward the end of his life, I talked with Paul Tillich about Christian imagery of immortality. Tillich's view was that the literal promise of an "afterlife" was a corrupt form of theological expression, disseminated among the relatively poor and uneducated. In the more profound expressions of this imagery, Tillich held, the idea of immortality symbolized unending spiritual continuity. Many, to be sure, would argue with this view, and it is undoubtedly more true at certain moments of history than others. But it does help us to grasp distinctions among different expressions of millennial thought.

When a millennial vision becomes so literalized that it is associated with a prediction of the actual end of the world on a particular day, on the basis of Biblical images or mathematical calculation applied to such images or whatever, we become aware of a disquieting border area of theology and psychopathology. Today in this country there are cults that claim Biblical imagery and attach it to nuclear danger, welcoming nuclear holocaust as a way of cleansing humankind of its sins. These groups maintain the fantasy that they, the true believers, will somehow survive. This of course is literalization, a renunciation of the regenerative dimensions of millennial imagery. The imagery of such cults may recall the schizophrenic person's paradoxical avoidance of annihilation by imagining a dead universe in which he or she is the last survivor.

Nuclear Winter and Nuclearism

Even worse, we bring a version of that debased millennialism to the weapons themselves. I have in mind the spiritual aberration that I call nuclearism: the exaggerated dependence upon, and even worship of, nuclear weapons. We embrace the weapons for purposes of safety and "security" and seek in them a means of keeping the world going, a form of salvation. Nuclear winter contributes additionally to our imagination by making it clear that the end point of nuclearism is extinction.

In his suggestively titled play *End of the World,* Arthur Kopit argues that it is the attraction to extinction that motivates the nuclearists in their dedication to scenarios of millions of dead and ultimately to the weapons themselves. That attraction is undoubtedly there for some: the Doctor Strangelove phenomenon of the "nuclear high," the seductive lure of the ultimate—that is, final—experience.

But more important, I believe, is the power over death and life perceived in the weapons, the investment we make in them as immortalizing objects. For they are capable of doing what in the past only God could do: destroy the world. In addition, the weapons represent an ultimate technology and therefore an object of our continuous and misguided efforts to solve or redeem with technology that which we find so difficult to solve or redeem in human arrangements. Nuclearism represents a terrible irony that only human beings could create: in our terror before the weapons and the fear and futurelessness they generate, we embrace these very potential agents of our annihilation and seek from them endless life-power. Nuclear winter heightens that absurdity and thereby contributes to our capacity to break this vicious circle of nuclearism.

The phenomenon I call the retirement syndrome—really retirement wisdom—illustrates both the pervasiveness of nuclearism and the rebellion against it. In 1982, when forced to retire at age eighty-one, Admiral Hyman B. Rickover, generally characterized as "the father of America's nuclear navy," said, "I think we'll probably destroy ourselves" and added, "I'm not proud of the part I played." One has to assume psychologically that the man-weapons constellation is so pervasive while a person is in office, the pattern of nuclearism so dominant, that the world is seen through a prism of nuclear weapons, and therefore nuclear weapons–centered policies are promulgated. At the moment of retirement, however, a person can take a step back and, prodded by conscience, voice doubts that were previously suppressed.

Of course Rickover was not the first. Eisenhower's famous warning about the military-industrial complex was a retirement speech. Others include J. Robert Oppenheimer, who initially favored using the bomb and blocked early scientific opposition to its use without warning on a populated city but later disowned responsibility for the second-generation H-bomb weapons system. Henry Stimson, Secretary of War at the time the bomb was first used, referred privately to the weapon as the "dreadful," the "awful," and the "diabolical." He even arranged to have available to him a subordinate whose main task was to listen to Stimson's pained concerns about the weapon. Yet he never wavered in his determination that the bomb should be used, and he arranged committee deliberations to suit his determination. Among his last acts before leaving office, however, was the drafting of a memorandum about the bomb in which he described it as "merely a first step in a control by man over the forces of nature too revolutionary and dangerous to fit into the old concept" and urged that we "enter into an arrangement with the Russians, the general purpose of which would be to control and limit the use of the atomic bomb as an instrument of war" (Alperovitz, 1965, pp. 276–279).

I am struck by the possibility of transformation away from nuclearism. That transformation is enhanced by confronting end-of-the-world imagery. Eugene Rabinowitz provides a very good example of just this possibility when he writes about the circumstances in which he and other nuclear scientists drafted one of the earliest petitions against the use of a nuclear weapon:

> In the summer of 1945, some of us walked the streets of Chicago vividly imagining the sky suddenly lit up by a giant fireball, the steel skeleton of skyscrapers bending into grotesque shapes and their masonry raining into the streets below, until a great cloud of dust rose and settled onto the crumbling city. (Rabinowitz, 1963, p. 156)

This image of the "end of the world" inspired him to urge his colleagues to return quickly to their work on the Franck Report, which he, Franck, Szilard, and a number of others in Chicago were instrumental in creating. To be sure, the report's recommendation that the atomic weapon not be used on a human population without warning was not heeded. But it has become a central document in our contemporary struggle to imagine the end of the world in order to preserve the world. Similar efforts of restitution, which restore symbols of human continuity to our numbed imaginations, are needed by the rest of us as well.

Nuclear winter becomes an important *imaginative* resource here. Just as we know that we must imagine our own death in order to live more fully, so must we now imagine the end of the world in order to take steps to maintain human existence.

References

Alperovitz, G. (1965). *Atomic diplomacy: Hiroshima and Potsdam.* New York: Simon & Schuster.

Glover, E. (1946). *War, sadism and pacifism.* London: George Allen & Unwin.

Hachiya, M. (1955). *Hiroshima diary.* Chapel Hill: University of North Carolina Press.

Lifton, R. J. (1983). *The broken connection* (chaps. 22, 23). New York: Basic Books. (Original work published 1979)

Lifton, R. J. (1984). *Death in life*. New York: Basic Books. (Original work published in 1968)

Mack, J. E. (1983). *Summary of general research findings*. Testimony to Select Committee, House of Representatives, U.S. Cong. Washington, DC: U.S. Government Printing Office.

Ota, Y. (1955). *Shikabane no machi* [Town of corpses]. Tokyo: Kawado Shobo.

Rabinowitz, E. (1963). Five years after. In M. Grodzins & E. Rabinowitz (Eds.), *The atomic age* (p. 156). New York: Basic Books.

Schreber, D. P. (1955). *Memoirs of my nervous illness* (I. Macalpine & R. A. Hunter, Eds. and Trans.). London: Wm. Dawson & Sons. (Original work published 1903)

National Security Reconsidered: New Perspectives Generated by the Prospect of a Nuclear Winter

JOHN E. MACK

Challenging Assumptions about National Security

The fact that man now has the capacity to destroy life as we know it on the planet was coming to be appreciated by many responsible people before the nuclear winter data became available late in 1983. In October 1982, for example, more than a year before the World after Nuclear War Conference at which the nuclear winter findings were made public, American Catholic bishops warned, "In the nuclear arsenals of the United States or the Soviet Union alone, there exists a capacity to do something no other age could imagine: we can threaten the created order." In their proposed letter on nuclear arms the bishops said, "Today the destructive potential of the nuclear powers threatens the sovereignty of God over the world He has brought into being. We could destroy His work" (American Catholic Bishops, 1982). The work of Richard Turco and his colleagues, building on the earlier findings of Paul Crutzen in Berlin and John Birks of Denver, demonstrated the profound, *unanticipated additional* effects that nuclear wars of varying sizes would have on the global atmosphere and the consequences of these effects for life on the planet (Turco et al., 1983; Sagan, 1983–84).

About seven years ago damage to the ozone layer of the atmosphere, and the consequent danger of penetrating ultraviolet radiation, was an earlier *unanticipated* discovery of an effect of nuclear detonations. As H. Jack Geiger has dryly commented, "We are entitled to wonder what other surprises lie ahead, what other devastating effects of nuclear war are as yet unknown and undescribed, since what we do not know about the effects of nuclear war is surely much greater than what we do know" (Geiger, 1984, p. 12). For three years we have been confronted with the likelihood that a nuclear war in which but a small fraction of the available destructive arsenals would be exploded could lead to a substantial lowering of the earth's temperatures with catastrophic consequences for life on the planet beyond those we had already expected.

But the discovery of these new dangers to the earth has had little impact on nuclear weapons policies in either the United States or the Soviet Union. A 1984 editorial in *Science* commented, "The completely new strategic implications of the nuclear winter scenarios have not yet received any great public attention or discussion" (Editorial, 1984). This is hardly less true in 1986. The nuclear superpowers maintain their hostile, ideologically grounded attitudes toward each other, seeking advantage where it can be seized, as if oblivious to the possibility that a nuclear war could start at any time through accident, miscalculation, direct attack, or escalation of a local or regional conflict. The purpose of this chapter is to examine our assumptions about national security and to explore the system of forces—psychological and institutional—that seem to hold us unswervingly on our present suicidal course.

By way of illustration of these forces, we might consider the forms taken by scientific debates about the nuclear winter data. For example, at a meeting of the Avoiding Nuclear War project at Harvard's Kennedy School in April 1984, scientists and other members of the strategic weapons community focused with intense interest upon the possible inaccuracies in the Turco-Sagan reports (Rathjens, 1984). "An order of magnitude of uncertainty" was disclosed as a result of possible miscalculation of the influence of rain and wind, and cooling at the ocean's edge. This discussion stressed different results, in the direction of somewhat less severity, that might be found using a "three-dimensional nine-layered noninteractive general circulation model" (Geiger, 1984). The possible political motivations of the TTAPS authors in using a computer model that would yield such a severe outcome were also scrutinized. Largely lost sight of among the scientists in the Kennedy School debate was the fact of nuclear war, its overwhelmingly catastrophic global consequences, and the additional dimension of disaster contained in the nuclear winter analysis.

Edward Zuckerman, author of *The Day after World War III* (1984), a book that details the government's plans for surviving a nuclear war, has pointed out the extent to which the debate on the severity of a nuclear winter and other post atomic war scenarios follows political lines. According to Zuckerman, those who oppose U.S. government nuclear weapons policies stress the worst consequences, whereas those who support the Reagan administration approach pursue a "life-will-go-on" line of argument and emphasize the uncertainties of all studies of the possible results of nuclear war. The Pentagon has commissioned its own studies. However, a preliminary report of one study funded by the Defense Department, which was undertaken through the National Academy of Sciences and chaired by Harvard science professor George Carrier, has largely confirmed the nuclear winter results. At a press conference on December 10, 1984, Professor Carrier said that his study's conclusions were for the most part consistent with the TTAPS report (Kaplan, 1984), although there are admitted uncertainties "plaguing all calculations of this phenomenon" and some of the effects might be milder (Katz, 1985).

It was also pointed out in the Kennedy School debate that there are strategic weapons analysts in the Department of Defense who wish to use the nuclear winter findings to argue *for* particular changes in nuclear strategy that would avoid a lowering of the earth's temperature—the use, for example, of smaller, more numerous, more accurate missiles and warheads, which would be likely to stir up less smoke and dust, or higher airbursts, which would incinerate surface structures and living creatures without sending into the atmosphere huge amounts of earth from craters that would be excavated by nuclear bursts near the ground.

But as Geiger has said, "These mindless, endless arguments about the technical details of temperature drops, particle rainouts, and computer models" distract our attention "from the fundamental fact, the fact that any nuclear war

would be a catastrophe without precedent in the history of
our species" (Geiger, 1984, p. 12). Zuckerman makes a similar point when he says:

> There is no need to hold to debatable—and thus dis-
> tracting—predictions of total doom to make a convincing
> case against nuclear war and against the policies of the
> Reagan administration and its predecessors that have
> made nuclear war more likely.
>
> For what if the debunkers of doomsday were some-
> how shown to be correct? What if we knew for a fact that
> the most wildly optimistic estimate of the effects of nu-
> clear war (that of Federal civil defense authorities) was
> accurate, and just 45 million Americans would be vapor-
> ized or burned to death or buried under collapsed build-
> ings or slashed by flying glass or condemned to a horri-
> ble lingering death from radiation sickness? And only 20
> or 30 million more would suffer sublethal radiation sick-
> ness or broken bones or disfiguring burns or other inju-
> ries? And only a few million of those who survived the
> war would die of cancer later? But the world would not
> end. And life would be nearly normal in Uruguay and
> New Zealand.
>
> Would nuclear war be acceptable then? Would there
> be any less need to rein in the arms race? (Zuckerman, 1984)

It would appear from this discussion that to a certain degree the data about nuclear winter—probably *any* data about
the effects of nuclear war—may be of less importance than
the points of view that particular weapons analysts and policymakers hold about the value of nuclear weapons in relation to strategic policies and superpower relations. These
policymakers, and perhaps *all* of us to a degree, wish to be
distracted from the central fact of the present nuclear age,
the overriding reality that now confronts mankind: our nuclear warheads and the ballistic missiles on which they are
mounted are failing to provide us with the security that is
their ostensible purpose. We remain completely exposed,
vulnerable to the intentions and plans of another nation. We

cannot, on our own, derive security from our nuclear systems, or perhaps from *any* military source, since nonnuclear wars carry the clear risk of escalating to nuclear ones. Although nuclear deterrence may—so far—have played a part in preventing a direct conflict between the superpowers, the balance of terror it represents cannot be expected to endure forever. Security based on nuclear deterrence may become ever more diminished, even as we seek to achieve it through new advances in nuclear weapons technology.

What, it may be asked, are the grounds for this assertion? It is based, simply, on the nature of nuclear weapons and their continent-crossing delivery systems. Before the nuclear age a nation's citizens had good reason to experience a sense of protection if they lived in a country with superior military forces as measured by numbers of potential combatants and the level of technological sophistication of the weaponry that might be used for offensive or defensive warfare. However devastating war might be to a nation's territories, however terrible the casualties, a militarily strong country had a reasonable hope of limiting its casualties and certainly of surviving with its homeland intact. Even in the worst of conflicts—as in the terrible destruction of the two world wars—the nations of the earth survived their ordeals as more or less the same entities they had been at the outset of the bloodshed, and the militarily superior forces achieved some sort of victory in the end.

But nuclear warheads, attached to international and intercontinental ballistic missiles, have made the notion of protection through superior military might obsolete. This is due not simply to the fact that these missiles can cross national boundaries as if at will, or even that no effective defense can be mounted against them, although these realities are part of what has changed. Rather, it is the shift in the order of magnitude of destructiveness of nuclear weapons as compared to all previous explosive devices and the interlocking nature of the offensive/defensive postures of the nuclear superpowers that have changed everything. Any use of nuclear weapons by one side now runs the risk of leading to planetary suicide by triggering an escalation process whose end point cannot be foreseen or controlled short of total destruction. Furthermore, we now live in the paradoxical situation in which nuclear military technological advances may actually *reduce* the security of the nation (and thus of all nations) that brings them into being. For the deployment of a weapons system that is superior by virtue of greater accuracy of delivery, proximity to the other nation's homeland, or difficulty of detection may, however "defensive" the intention has been, be seen by the other side as an aggressive threat against which it could feel impelled to strike preemptively in order not to be attacked first (Lebow, 1985).

A moment's reflection will support this point. Consider the reaction of the American administration to the Soviet's placing of SS-20 missiles in European Russia, or the Soviet response to the deployment of the Pershing II missiles in West Germany. In each instance the nation deploying the new system claimed to regard its action as purely defensive, intended to improve or modernize an old system or to right a previous imbalance. Yet the opposing nation regarded the action as an intolerable and threatening move. Indeed, we may be fortunate to have survived as long as we have when one considers the degree of distrust and fear that obtains between the nuclear superpowers.

Despite protestations to the contrary, there is considerable evidence that the new reality created by nuclear weapons— or, more accurately, the reality that *we* have evolved for ourselves by creating nuclear weapons—has had very little impact on the way policymakers in the United States think about such matters as strength, war, deterrence, and defense. On the contrary, arguments for particular policy alternatives, and the policies themselves, reflect anachronistic attitudes, what psychiatrist Jerome Frank calls a prenuclear mentality. One of the "antinuclear" admirals interviewed by Frank, a retired officer who had actually seen thermonuclear test explosions in the Pacific Ocean, made the point bluntly: "Practically none of the policymakers, let alone the staff that supports them, has any real feeling for what these weapons are. In a quite literal use of language, they don't know what they're talking about" (Frank, 1984, p. 34). Similarly, prenuclear ideas about deterrence have been carried forward by bizarre extrapolations into the nuclear context. Terms like *resolve* and *credibility* may be used without careful attention to what they must mean in the nuclear context—namely, the maintenance of a convincing attitude of apparent willingness to risk the destruction of most if not all life on the planet to support nationalistic interests (see Lebow, 1985).

A failure to appreciate the new reality brought about by nuclear technology can lead to arguments for one or another detail of a nuclear weapons policy that can seem quite absurd if one lives outside the system of thought from which the reasoning springs. I have, for example, heard the U.S. government's opposition to a comprehensive nuclear test ban treaty defended with the argument that underground testing can yield useful information about how various sorts of shields attached to tanks might withstand nuclear explosions, and that such protection of tanks would be part of a credible deterrence—that is, by eliminating a possible perception by the Soviets of "weakness" in American defensive capability. In this argument prenuclear and nuclear physical realities are mingled without distinction. Tanks, we are being asked to believe, can be made safe from nuclear destruction. The argument for an antiballistic missile defense system based in space (Star Wars, SDI, BMD) is, in my view, another expression of prenuclear thinking, reflecting a kind of a nostalgia, a sentimental longing for an earlier time when a nation could protect itself militarily by technically more advanced military defenses.

The failure to grasp fully the new reality with which we must now contend may be making us more vulnerable and insecure. Before proceeding further it may be useful to consider the several connotations of *national security*. These words imply a network of military and political institutions and associated activities through which the United States, or any government, seeks to protect its people. They also seem to refer to the perceived success of that system, in the sense of:

do we "have" national security? Or more simply, are we "secure"? The effectiveness of measures for achieving national security have conventionally been tested or judged by their results, such as success in preventing war, the limitation of loss of life or destruction in combat, or outcomes of victory or defeat. In the case of nuclear weapons, there can be no testing in action of the system, nor can we turn to any relevant historical war experience. The measure of security then becomes a matter of judgment.

Objective estimates are difficult. They include such uncertainties as the assessment of the level of international tensions, predictions of the likelihood of nuclear war, the chances of its escalation should a small nuclear war begin, or the possibility of surviving one. Because the estimation of these intangibles is so uncertain we are led to rely on more subjective criteria in judging the success or failure of national security policies. Security then becomes a state of mind. Nuclear weapons analyst Larry Smith, now at the Kennedy School, made this point quite simply. "Security," he said, "is being able to go to bed at night unafraid" (Smith, 1983). By this criterion there is considerable evidence that many people in the United States and other countries, while crediting the role of nuclear deterrence in preventing a major war between the United States and the Soviet Union, recognize their vulnerability to nuclear attack and experience considerable concern about the future.

Polls conducted by Yankelovich, Skelly, and White in 1984 revealed that 38 percent of the American people believed that an all-out nuclear war was likely to occur in the next ten years, and 68 percent agreed that "if both sides keep building missiles instead of negotiating to get rid of them, it is only a matter of time before they are used" (Yankelovich & Doble, 1984, p. 37). At the same time, 89 percent subscribed to the view that there can be "no winner: in an all-out nuclear war both the United States and the Soviet Union would be completely destroyed," and 83 percent said that "we cannot be certain that life on earth will continue after a nuclear war" (p. 34). Young people in particular seem vulnerable to the perceived threat of nuclear war. Fifty percent of those under thirty polled by Yankelovich expected that an all-out nuclear war would occur in the next ten years. In his address to the nation on November 22, 1982, on nuclear strategy toward the Soviet Union, President Reagan expressed his concern "about the effects the nuclear fear is having on our people." He spoke of letters he was receiving from schoolchildren that were "often full of terror" (Reagan, 1982). Studies conducted in the United States, the Soviet Union, Finland, and several other countries between 1978 and 1984 revealed the fears and insecurities of children and adolescents in relation to the nuclear threat. A considerable percentage of these young people expect to die in a nuclear war (Beardslee & Mack, 1982, 1983; Bachman, 1983; Solantaus et al., 1983; Chivian & J. Goodman, 1984; L. Goodman et al., 1983; Stoddard & Mack, 1985). Judging by the actual experience of children and adults in relation to the nuclear threat, there is little support for President Reagan's claim made early in 1984 that America's policy of deterrence "is making the world a safer place. Safer because now there is less danger that the Soviet leadership will underestimate our strength or question our resolve" (Reagan, 1984).

Statements made by American teenagers on questionnaires and interviews between 1978 and 1983 revealed their perplexity in relation to the protection offered by nuclear weapons. On the one hand, some express the view that they would not wish to live in a situation in which the Soviet Union had nuclear weapons and the United States did not. At the same time some teenagers say bluntly that they experience very little safety or protection from nuclear weapons and feel more insecure than secure. The following statements are characteristic of those made by adolescents in the Boston area on this subject:

—Nuclear weapons are a direct threat to our national security and to world peace, and to all human life.
—As long as the superpowers keep making nuclear weapons, then there is a need for our nation to possess them too.

—How can you call protection building weapons that will destroy not only the Soviet Union but the United States also?
—They make me feel more threatened than safe. We have weapons. They have weapons. It's just a matter of who fires first. That's it.
—All the missiles and stuff like that. . . . It makes me feel more scared 'cause Russia's going to have the same thing. And other countries that oppose you are going to have the same thing.
—People want security, and this is the ultimate insecurity. It isn't even death; it's ultimate destruction.
—I think trying to preserve peace with bombs is like forcing someone to love you by threatening them with rape. . . . Something like peace and security and love doesn't come under pressure.

This last point—the futility in the nuclear age of seeking one's own security by threatening someone else's—has been echoed by Jerome Frank's antinuclear admirals (Frank, 1984). One of them told him, "The most overriding problem that I can see is that we believe we can solve our problems by threatening or even using nuclear weapons." Another said, "We have to change our definition of what security is. You don't get security by building someone else's insecurity."

If, then, the continued superpower nuclear weapons competition deepens a sense of insecurity among the people we are seeking to protect, why do we persist in this dangerous and vain pursuit? Psychologist Steven Kull has suggested that our leaders, who define their responsibilities largely in nationalistic terms, pursue with the compliance of the citizenry the *illusion* of security through nuclear weapons precisely because we are so powerless, because we feel there is nothing else we can do, and because we find this reality unbearable. "In the face of this unsettling situation," Kull writes, "it certainly is appealing to create the *feeling* that there is some meaningful action that would, however meagerly, enhance our security" (Kull, 1984). We *want* to believe President Reagan that we are safer as a result of his policies, even though at a deeper level we may know that we are not.

Our attitude toward civil defense is consistent with Kull's hypothesis. Even though we and the Soviets know from objective study that there can be no significant or useful protection from nuclear attack, our two governments persist in spending money on civil defense programs that cannot be effective. Some of our own children scoff at civil defense measures (Goodman et al., 1983), and a group of Russian children interviewed in 1983 stated bluntly that shelters would do nothing to ensure their survival (Chivian & Goodman, 1984). A Soviet physician at the 1982 Congress of International Physicians for the Prevention of Nuclear War acknowledged that the Soviet government cannot admit to its people that it has no way to protect them in the event of a nuclear war. The American government may be similarly motivated in promulgating civil defense planning through the Federal Emergency Planning Agency.

If it is true that we persist in the quest for security through more and better nuclear weapons, knowing all the while that we are powerless, vulnerable, and defenseless in the face of the current nuclear deadlock, why do we continue on this futile and dangerous course?

I offer three assumptions. First, except for a small group of extreme millennialists who welcome nuclear war as the fulfillment of the Biblical prophecy of Armageddon (and these individuals are, I suspect, driven by fears they do not comprehend), all human beings wish to prevent nuclear war. Second, no one willfully and knowingly pursues activities he holds to be destructive or evil, however much others may suffer as a result of particular policies or actions; rather, we explain to ourselves what we do in terms of some positive set of human values. In the case of nuclear weapons, for example, we may decide that the risks of planetary destruction we are assuming are "worth it" in order to prevent the possibility of Soviet expansion or conquest. Third, if the pattern of forces that perpetuate the nuclear weapons competition could be accurately revealed in such a way as to account for the seemingly irrational behavior of the nuclear superpowers—irrational if we accept that our present course is dangerous and threatening to life when our intention is to preserve it—

and if practical alternatives could be made available to the leaders of these powers, they would readily embrace them, and their citizens would support the new initiatives.

It is, of course, possible that the pattern of forces might be revealed without alternatives being offered or that new possibilities will be pursued by our leaders before the sources of our predicament are fully understood. I am presuming, however, that there is a close relationship between scientific and other forms of knowledge and policy-making in the nuclear arms race as in any other political context.

A number of writers have applied the concept of addiction to try to explain this phenomenon. Substance abuse expert Howard Shaffer first brought this way of looking at the nuclear arms race to my attention in a letter of October 1, 1983. He suggested that we might think of "nuclear arms development, implementation and use as an addictive behavior pattern." Like addicts, Shaffer went on to suggest, the leaders of the nuclear powers are seeking to "achieve an emotional state that existed many years ago." They "engage in behaviors which were once useful in spite of the concurrent dangers." Novelist Kurt Vonnegut wrote in an article, "I am persuaded that there are among us people who are tragically hooked on preparations for war. . . . I mean it. I am not joking. Compulsive preparers for World War III, in this country or any other, are as tragically and, yes, as repulsively addicted as any stockbroker passed out with his head in a toilet in the Port Authority bus terminal" (Vonnegut, 1983).

Steven Kull writes, "We have become like drug addicts, hooked on a quick fix of illusory security through methods that actually undermine our security" (Kull, 1984, p. 24). Former ambassador to the Soviet Union George Kennan has extended the idea of addiction to our whole society's relationship to nuclear weapons. Kennan suggests, more clearly than any writer of his stature has done before, that the nuclear weapons competition has a driving power of its own, independent of whatever justification for it the Soviet Union may provide:

The habit of spending from two to three hundred billions of dollars annually on preparations for an imagined
war with Russia—a habit reaching deeply into the lives
and interests of millions of our citizens both in and out
of the armed services, including industrial workers, labor
union officials, politicians, legislators, and middlemen:
this habit has risen to the status of a vast addiction of
American society, an addiction whose overcoming would
encounter the most intense resistance and take years to
accomplish even if the Soviet Union had in the meantime
miraculously disappeared from the earth. (Kennan, 1984, p.
78)

The metaphor of addiction may be valuable for understanding the nuclear weapons competition in certain respects. It describes its compulsive quality, the seemingly
headlong continuity despite the dangers we know so well. It
captures the quality of intense attachment, the neutralization
of disturbing feelings, and the application of outdated concepts of strength and power.

But the analogy to addiction is also imprecise. In the case
of an individual addict, we are more or less clear as to where
the problem resides. But in the case of the nuclear weapons
competition, who or what is addicted? Shaffer and Vonnegut say it is certain leaders; Kennan implies that it is the whole
society. Kull does not really say. More important, the addiction metaphor does not identify the forces, analogous to the
biological and psychological drives and affects with which we
are familiar in chemical addictions, that give the nuclear
weapons competition its compelling power. The remaining
pages of this chapter will be devoted to identifying these forces
and to suggesting alternatives that grow out of such understanding.

Habits of Power and Power Relationships

Teenagers, when they talk about the causes of the arms
race, often recognize the desire for power, dominance, and

strength as being among its principal driving forces (Goodman et al., 1984; Snow, 1984). Andrew Schmookler has analyzed the central role of power in the evolution of social systems, including the relationships among nations (1984). Power
motivations are present in all the vested interests discussed
later in this chapter. The extraordinary explosive power and
destructiveness of nuclear weapons endows them with a particular power-enhancing dimension for those who seem to
have identified with this property. Power seems to provide
the emotional fuel that drives the whole system.

   In considering the operation of power in international relations, who, or what, is to be considered its focus: an individual? the nation? some other group or groups? now one,
now another, or sometimes all of these? We might locate
power in a group, institution, or system. Would the power
that interests us then be the individual's desire for and acquisition of influence, dominance, and control within the
framework and ideology of the national group in question?
But the power that concerns us, the power that is really *powerful,* is the linkage of the individual who has a strong power
drive with other similar individuals and with an institution,
especially a military organization or a nation, that has nonhuman *physical* power which it can use destructively. Power,
as Schmookler has written, may be "a function of superior
organization" (1984, p. 255). This seems about as far as we
can go: power is located in an individual-group system. In
the special case of nations in relation to other nations, power
can be used defensively and to control aggression or, aggres-
sively, to dominate, control, and destroy other nations.

   Power seems to have an intimate connection with security
and survival. The individual may seek political power to off-
set a deep personal sense of weakness and insecurity. As
Schmookler has shown convincingly, the historical survival of
nations has depended traditionally on power—the power to
dominate with force other peoples and countries. Individuals, feeling weak generally in relation to the larger human
and nonhuman forces that surround them, have traditionally looked to some large group entity—an organization, a

nation, or an empire—to protect them from attack or to
overcome their inner sense of vulnerability and powerlessness. We often derive our sense of power from identification
with leaders who appear powerful by virtue of their apparent willingness to use the military strength of the nation
against other nations perceived as threatening. Indeed, national leaders are, as Schmookler has written, "selected for
power," having themselves survived the ordeals that along the
way select out less power-oriented individuals. Much of Ronald Reagan's popularity is tied to the public's perception of
him as a strong leader, willing to "stand up to" or "not be
pushed around by" the Russians and to use American military power to protect our security or defend our "national
interests." At the same time Reagan is also perceived by many
thoughtful people in the United States and other countries
as a dangerous leader because of his apparent unwillingness
or inability to grasp fundamental changes in the meaning of
power and security that have come about as a result of the
nature of nuclear weapons and their delivery systems.

A number of questions now confront mankind in relation
to power. One obvious question is whether the gratifications
of power—apparently a fundamental psychological need of
human beings functioning individually or in groups—can be
experienced in a nonnationalistic context. Do the satisfactions of political power depend upon identification with a
group or nation that dominates other groups, especially
through military force or superiority? The national self-esteem that seems to accrue to being militarily powerful—
"Number One" in the sports jargon that permeates American politics—appears to be deeply rooted in the collective
emotional life of many societies. Can equivalent human needs
and satisfactions be gained supranationally, by seeking the
common security of all nations, or through international col-
laborative action to solve the host of nonmilitary problems
that confront mankind?

British military historian B. H. Liddell Hart, in an obitu-
ary essay on T. E. Lawrence, remarked upon his friend's
freedom from ambition, "especially from the lust of power."

"His power," Liddell Hart continued, "sprang from knowledge and understanding, not from position. His influence was
free of domination" (Lawrence, 1963). It remains to be seen
whether the satisfactions of power derived from sources other
than domination and the use of force can gain the upper hand
in relations among the nuclear nations before we all fall victim to the anachronisms of traditional military thinking.

The Role of Vested Interests in Perpetuating the Nuclear Weapons Competition

Jerome B. Wiesner, science adviser to Presidents Kennedy
and Johnson, writes, "Hundreds of thousands of individuals
with a vested interest in the arms race work full-time fostering it" (1984, p. 30). Wiesner's statement is certainly true, but
one may consider "vested interest" in a broader sense, to include not only direct profit or personal gain but also attachment to ideas, points of view, or ways of looking at the world,
especially at the relationships between nations. By a vested
interest I have in mind any human attachment, involvement,
commitment, emotional investment, or psychological energy
that may contribute to the continuation of the nuclear weapons competition. I have divided vested interests into economic, political, career-professional, technological, and col-
lective-psychological or philosophical (embodied in the term
ideology). These various investments provide powerful sources
of resistance to change in relation to the nuclear weapons
competition (Mack, 1984). I will touch only briefly on the first
four, stressing collective psychology or ideology because this
is my area of interest and also because I believe that ideological structures justify or sustain all the other interests.

From the *economic* standpoint, nuclear-related industries
support millions of jobs and return huge profits to corporate
executives and investors. Yet there is evidence that removal
of the moral justification for nuclear weapons work—as has
occurred in the case of nuclear engineers at General Electric,
employees at the Pantex Plant in Amarillo, Texas, which

makes nuclear bombs, and workers constructing missile guidance systems at Draper Labs—may make continued nuclear weapons-related work personally untenable for many individuals. Similarly, there are situations in which corporate leaders, when they once confront the effects of what they are doing or question the validity of the justification for it, speak out—often after retirement—against the arms race and begin to work toward ending it.

By *political* vested interests I have in mind the habit of American party leaders of maintaining for domestic political purposes the sort of hostile attitude toward the Soviet Union that sustains our part in the nuclear arms race. A comparable set of attitudes, viewed as necessary for keeping political power internally, may be maintained by Soviet leaders. McGeorge Bundy, reviewing a quarter century of American presidential elections, said during the 1984 campaign that all candidates seem to have felt a necessity to speak distrustfully of the Russians and appear militarily "strong," which usually has meant a relatively unquestioning support of huge expenditures on defense. As a result serious discussion of the underlying issues has yet to take place within the American government (Bundy, 1984). As if in confirmation of Bundy's experience, the American people were treated in the second 1984 presidential debate to the depressing spectacle of the Democratic candidate appearing even more untrusting, belligerent, and bellicose toward the Soviet Union than his Republican opponent.

The fact that there are scientific, academic, political, military, and other *careers* to be made in nuclear weapons–related work is, of course, familiar to everyone. I am referring here to the intellectual or technical interest and excitement about the problems involved as well as the economic rewards. Many nuclear weapons-related problems are considered scientifically interesting—"sweet," in the argot of the field. But once again this work requires a moral justification, a worthy enemy, to make it tolerable or seem worthwhile. Individuals involved in the more purely technocratic aspect may be less inclined to question what they are doing, and more likely to carry out their jobs with relatively little thought about the use to which their products will be put.

Lisa Peattie, professor of Urban Anthropology at MIT, has stressed the way in which the specialization of industrial tasks, in the case of the nuclear arms race as in the development of the gas chamber industry in Hitler's Germany, has resulted in a surrender of personal responsibility (Peattie, 1984). "Organizational specialization," she writes, supported by fragmented thinking (Mack, 1985), produces "differential rewards." According to Peattie, "specialization brings with it the possibility of developing the peculiarly human satisfactions"—and, I would add, satisfaction without responsibility—"in problem-solving, expertise and the exercise of skills" (p. 35). Since the early 1950s the nuclear arms race has spawned an entirely new professional/technical/academic industry or career path, that of nuclear "strategic expert." Once the task of preventing nuclear war is defined as occurring by means of strategic thinking within the parameters of a given system, it is unlikely that much attention will be given to questioning the system itself.

The investment of our society in *technological* solutions and advances is related closely to career opportunities but has a power and dynamic of its own. As psychiatrist Joel Kovel has said, modern man is "swaddled" in technology from the day of birth. He *worships* technology. "It becomes his *alter* mother, a cocoon that carries him passively through the world, as visitors to Florida's Disney World are encased in a plexiglas vessel and wafted before the universe's wonders" (1983, p. 95). Death itself has been robbed of its emotional power and dignity as real war killings on television have become largely indistinguishable from fictional melodramas, and human organisms for whom no existence in a meaningful sense remains are kept alive by the artificial power of machines.

Most (to me) reasonable people seem to have thought that the Star Wars antiballistic missile defense scheme would have been laughed out of existence by its sheer absurdity when viewed from any number of angles—economic, strategic, psychological, technical, moral, and practical. But such thoughts fail to reckon with the depth of the public's gullibility and blind faith in technological solutions to human problems. President Reagan understood better the power of this faith when combined with the citizenry's terrible fear of nuclear attack by the Soviet Union. "Let me share with you a vision of the future which offers hope," he said in the famous March 23, 1983, speech on "A New Defense" (1984). "Let us turn to the very strengths in technology that spawned our great industrial base and that have given us the quality of life we enjoy today. . . . What if free people could live secure in the knowledge that their security did not rest upon the threat of instant U.S. retaliation to deter a Soviet attack?" The Star Wars plan is regarded as impractical, unfeasible, and unwise by the great majority of the American scientific community. But the arguments of these scientists have not prevailed against the appeal to blind faith contained in the president's vision, which is supported only by Edward Teller and a few other scientists. Reason, we know, has never fared well when pitted against faith, especially when faith is driven by terror.

Nuclear weapons, principally because of their cosmic explosive power, seem to exert a hypnotic hold on certain people. Energy Secretary James Edwards found nuclear test explosions "exciting." A young woman acknowledged in a community discussion group, after seeing the television film "The Day After," that she found it "thrilling" to see the missiles soaring out of their silos in the Kansas cornfields (Mack, 1983). A California cab driver thought a major war would be "terribly exciting." A poet in Philadelphia believes a nuclear explosion has "a kind of staggering beauty" (Carey, 1983a).

We have little systematic knowledge of the emotional relationship of nuclear strategists, weapons designers, and others to the weapons themselves. We often read statements by policymakers of their horror of the bomb. We know less about the ways, suggested in statements by Oppenheimer, Teller, and others, in which they have embraced the weapons, beginning with the assignment of pet names like "Fat Man" and "Little Boy" to the first bombs. Machines, as Kovel points out, may extend the power of our bodies. But nuclear warheads on ballistic missiles seem to multiply this power infinitely. Novelist Edith Wharton wrote from France during World War I, "It is one of the most detestable things about war that everything connected with it, except the death and ruin that result, is such a heightening of life, so visually stimulating and absorbing" (Lewis, 1975, p. 376). In 1982 an issue of *Life* magazine was devoted to illustrations of our new missiles on land, at sea, and in the air—sleek and colorful, splendid in their suggested power. Nowhere in the article was there even a hint of the destructive properties of these projectiles or what they would be used for. Perhaps we have within us a new form of war loving and have bred a new sort of war lover, spellbound by the possibility of a nuclear Armageddon. It is now the superpower of the bomb, the strange fruit of modern technology, through which they and we have linked ourselves to the primal force of the universe, concentrated in our limited mortal hands only upon destruction.

And—I think it is important that we face this fact—it is American technological exuberance and dynamism, what national security expert Nancy Ramsey has called our "lust for technological one-upsmanship" (1984), that have shown the way among the nations of the world. It is we who have used the bomb; we who have led at virtually every step of the arms race; we who have most often rejected treaties to curb nuclear proliferation. Yes, Soviet militarism has been our excuse, but I would argue that it is an insufficient one. The enthusiasm with which we have developed nuclear weapons technology, creating ever more sophisticated weapons systems, cannot be accounted for by the Russian threat alone, a threat that may have been made more dangerous by our initiatives, as the Soviets have felt compelled to respond to each advance of ours with a matching escalation of their own. Nuclear physicist Herbert York is one of the few American scientists to have assigned responsibility for the dangers of escalation to the impetus of American technology. He writes:

> The reason for our leading the world in this mad rush toward the ultimate absurdity . . . is not that our leaders

have been less sensitive to the dangers of the arms race, it is not that our leaders are less wise, it is not that we are more aggressive or less concerned about the dangers to the rest of mankind. Rather, the reasons are that we are richer and more powerful, that our science and technology are more dynamic, that we generate more ideas of all kinds. (York, 1970, pp. 238–239)

There is another aspect of advanced technology that is especially dangerous. It seals off its creator or the person who uses it from its consequences or effects. This isolation is both physical and emotional. The pediatrician in a neonatal intensive care unit is separated by tubes and plastic bubbles from the infants he is treating. The missile launcher at the bottom of a Minuteman silo would never see the havoc he would cause if he sent his missile on its way. Similarly, the weapons designer at Livermore Laboratory, or the nuclear strategist at Harvard or in the Pentagon, not only is physically removed from the weapons on planes, in submarines, or in silos but may be emotionally remote from the devastation that would result from their use. The strategist may seek an especially great emotional distance from the subject of his work precisely because the weapons are so unfathomably destructive. Physical and emotional distancing permits a surrender of responsibility on the part of leaders and public alike in relation to nuclear weapons—leaders because they seem unable to look fully at what the weapons do and the related disproportion between the national "interests" they are supposed to serve and the consequences of their actual use; the general public because they are awed by the technology itself, feel powerless, and thus exempt themselves from participation in the policy-making process.

Compelling as all of these elements may be, none of them, alone or in combination, could sustain the nuclear arms race without a system of thought, a special way of looking at the play of forces in the domain of international relations and international conflict. This framework must operate at both a collective and an individual level. It thus permeates a whole society. It is psychopolitical—comprising the thoughts and

emotions that underlie the political process—and psycho-
philosophical insofar as it is reflective of the mind's way of
apprehending reality where relationships among ethnic and
national groups are concerned. I will use the term *ideology* to
capture what I have in mind, although I am using it in a
broader, more general sense than the way in which it is ordinarily employed. I refer not only to specific political and
economic thought systems but to the *tendency* of the mind or
self in its political dimension to form ideologies. As creatures
involved in the power relationships of human groups, we
create ideologies as plants bring forth shoots. By ideology in
the international political arena, I mean the tendency of a
nation, or group of nations, to create and operate according
to a framework of assumptions, both conscious and uncon-
scious, that determines its view of its own and other nations'
political behavior, motivation, and intentions.

International political ideologies seem at first to be the
special property of a nation's leaders, who, trained to think
nationalistically, then supposedly indoctrinate their citizenry.
But this is too simple a view. It is true, of course, that a particular leader may, on the basis of his personal psychological
history and emotional needs, have a predilection for an extreme expression of a particular ideology—a right-wing
American of a virulent form of anticommunism or a Soviet
leader of a rabid brand of anticapitalism. But a prevailing
ideology has a deeper and broader basis. It exists in a nation
as a kind of atmosphere, a historical habit or potential, manifest or latent in both the ordinary citizenry and the leadership, deriving from that country's political and religious history and cultural traditions. American anti-Sovietism, for
example, has roots not only in the realities of Soviet expansion and opportunism since World War II but also in our
traditions of frontier freedom, economic opportunity, Christian dualism, and nineteenth-century anti-Russian feeling,
among other sources. For a leader like Ronald Reagan, ideology is a kind of rich national political reservoir into which
he can dip in order to connect his private psychology with
the emotional fears and needs of the people, at the same time

adapting this psychopolitical ensemble to contemporary international political exigencies.

I use the word *exigency* rather than *reality* because the assessment of political reality is so subjective, and more important, the power of ideology to determine the perception of international political actualities can override most facts. In the face of extreme ideological positions, what is possible for one nation to perceive in relation to another nation's people, culture, and political behavior is narrowly circumscribed by its own ideological structures. One's own country's military actions will inevitably be seen as justified on the grounds of defense and security; the other nation's moves will be seen as inexcusably provocative or aggressive.

The Ideologies of Enmity and the Soviet-American Relationship

Ideological structures create the need for enemies and determine how enemies are viewed. They do not, at least by themselves, determine *who* will become enemies; this is the result of historical circumstances that become fitted to ideological thought structures. The need for enemies grows out of the dichotomizing tendency of the child's mind (Pinderhughes, 1982; Volkan, 1984). From infancy the human organism experiences a vast range of encounters with human and nonhuman objects in the outside world, which he divides for his own survival into the safe and the unsafe, friend and alien, ally and enemy, good and evil. To these objects, beginning with the parents, siblings, and other family members, the child may also attribute by displacement or projection his own hostile or loving impulses, perceiving the other as if it were a mirror of his own emotional life. This dichotomizing tendency becomes organized within the family into a set of perceptions that determine the relationship among peoples, including ethnic and national groups. A child growing up learns—usually sometime between ages six and ten—which peoples he can trust or love and which he is expected to hate or fear. The child's political and ideological educa-

tion will continue in school and also through the indoctri-
nation to which he is inevitably exposed in the mass media.
Television in particular, through its brief, oversimplified,
dramatic coverage of complex political events, its evocative
reliance on violent images, and the control of the major net-
works by the society's ruling elite, tends to reinforce the dichotomizing tendency of the child's mind as it perpetuates
itself in the adult. Television thus becomes a powerful force
for the communication, if not the actual creation, of primitive ideological thinking.

The ideologies of enmity have certain easily recognized
characteristics. Through them the enemy government and
people's qualities and behavior tend to be devalued. The enemy's destructive acts are highlighted in the media and its
positive qualities go unreported. Sometimes a distinction is
drawn between a people and its government, creating a new
dichotomy through which the enemy government can be de-
picted as even more evil than before. Demonization and de-
humanization are extreme forms of ideological devaluation,
which seem to occur especially when a country intends to make
war against another people. The enemy is demonized in order to be able to present a sufficient picture of evil to the
public at home, and dehumanized so that the adversary's
population can be killed without guilt. Erik Erikson has introduced the term *pseudospeciation* to describe the tendency
of one people to depict another as so lacking in human qualities as to seem not to belong to the human race at all (1969
and in this book).

The language of enmity recurs with monotonous regular-
ity through the pages of history. The names of the protago-
nists change, but the words they use to describe each other
remain the same (Frank, 1982). The enemy is invariably
uniquely vicious, treacherous, and cruel. One's own people
are progressive, courageous, and virtuous. One's own country's brutalities, if perceived or acknowledged at all, are justified by the ideological struggle, but the enemy's behavior is
wantonly brutal and its justifications are dismissed as propaganda. The ideologies of enmity act as lenses or, more ac-

curately, blinders, which determine what is possible for one nation to see about another. None of this is meant to imply that there are not important moral distinctions to be made among nations in their behavior toward one another. I am arguing simply that a nation engaged in an adversarial struggle to which it is economically, politically, and ideologically deeply committed is in a poor position to make such distinctions.

In the twentieth century virtually all the powerful nations have participated directly or indirectly in mass killing, political assassination, terrorism, covert wars fought through surrogates, economic exploitation, and deadly bombing of civilian populations. In each instance, a nation's prevailing ideology, linked to its definition of its own interests or security, is given as the justification. Styles differ. One nation may be more sadistic or directly brutal. We Americans seem to clothe our actions in moral pieties, even as we subvert the values we proclaim. British writer Timothy Garton Ash, comparing Soviet policies in Eastern Europe and American policies in Central America, found less moral distinction than he had expected when he began to investigate the subject. "Many Western Europeans," he notes, "object less to the substance of U.S. policy toward Central America than to the moralistic rhetoric in which it is presented" (1984). "We Americans are sentimental murderers," says Alaskan journalist Michael Carey; "we kill people for their own good" (1983b).

Perhaps a first step toward a political maturity that is adapted to the contemporary interdependency of the world's nations would be to recognize the blinders ideologies place on our ability to make accurate moral distinctions. It might be useful to learn how ideologies serve as lenses through which a nation distorts the world around it, excuses murderous behavior of its own, and ultimately subverts the values it professes and that its policies are said to uphold. I believe George Kennan had something like this in mind when he wrote about the United States in relation to nuclear arms control, "We will have to look more closely at ourselves—at our own motiva-

tion, our own behavior, the formative processes of our own
society—than we have to date" (1984).

The current ideological enemy of the United States is the
Soviet Union—not communism, for we are busy establishing
positive ties with China and other Marxist countries. It is less
clear that the United States is the focus of Soviet hostility and
ideological fixation to the same single-minded degree, as the
Soviet Union must also deal with the threat of China. I am
writing, of course, from an American perspective. An analogous discussion might take place from a Soviet point of view.

The shibboleth of "national security," which may be translated as military expenditure and preparedness to fight an
imagined war with the Soviet Union, is the underlying justification for all the American vested interests described above.
Virtually the entire structure of economic reward, national
political power, career advancement, and progress in nuclear weapons technology rests on a base of anti-Sovietism, a
simplified division of the world into friends and enemies,
Eastern and Western camps, locked in deadly ideological
combat. Without this structure of enmity the justification for
the trillion-dollar military-industrial system, and the array of
rewards it returns at all levels of our society, would be removed. Presumably the need for "security" in the face of U.S.
militarism provides the basis for a comparable array of rewards in the Soviet Union, but fear of China is a complicat-
ing dimension.

But the Soviet Union *is* aggressive, *is* a military threat, it
may justifiably be argued. Look at its murderous behavior in
Afghanistan, the brutal suppression of Eastern Europe, the
support of revolutions in Africa and Central America, and
the expanding nuclear weapons arsenal. The Soviet Union *is*
a formidable power and *does* threaten our security. This may
be true, but I would argue that what we know about the way
ideology determines perception should make us suspicious of
the degree to which it is true or what it is possible for us to
see. To what extent, for example, does our multidetermined
investment in keeping the Soviet Union as the enemy, maintaining it as the justification for the many rewards already

described, shape what we can possibly know of Soviet behavior and intentions? History has taught us that once an ideological frame is established the nation selected as an adversary provides no shortage of actions conforming to the expectation of evil that is the essence of the ideological mindset.

It is rare for Americans to consider how our own initiatives drive Soviet behavior, *creating* the USSR as the enemy, in conformity with our anti-Soviet ideology, in order to perpetuate the structures and rewards described above. We seldom ask to what degree American and Soviet military initiatives perpetuate a cycle of fear and distrust so intimately interconnected that responsibility cannot be assigned to one power separate from the other. To what extent do our self-fitted ideological lenses keep us ignorant of the destruction to life and hope that our own policies wreak abroad while we justify them at home through slogans of freedom and liberty— the real benefits of which, insofar as they still exist anywhere, are reserved for domestic enjoyment? To what extent do our principal media present a consciously and unconsciously distorted view of the Soviet Union, focusing on negative aspects while United States–supported depredations and exploitations are largely ignored—the kinds of distortion we attribute to the mass media of nondemocratic societies? Until these questions are explored further, I will not try to provide answers. But we might, in the meantime, at least maintain greater suspicion regarding the limitations our ideological thought patterns impose on the objectivity of our vision.

The vested interests that sustain the arms race in the nuclear nations are also embodied in an extensive, interlocking system of institutions whose decisions are made largely outside the public's view (Oxford Research Group, 1984). In the United States, private and military weapons laboratories, industrial corporations, universities, government agencies, and the military services have evolved into a complex, interdependent system for nuclear weapons acquisition in which decision-making authority is widely diffused. Through this system, promoted at all levels by the rationale of "national security" and sustained by the ideology of East-West polarization and anti-Sovietism, economic rewards are delivered, political power is granted, careers are made, and technological advances are achieved.

By the time the public becomes aware of a new weapons system through a speech by the president or the secretary of defense, or through debate over funding in the Congress, decisions concerning weapon design, production, procurement by the service branches, and even deployment have already been made. So much money has been spent, and so many careers have been made or are about to be made, that a momentum has been established that is difficult to reverse. The evocation of the Soviet threat by the president, key cabinet members, or top military leaders is generally enough to stifle dissent in the Congress, many of whose members have their own vested interests in particular weapons systems in their states, sometimes despite the fact that their personal judgment may tell them that the nuclear device is of no value and might even be harmful. Great Britain, the Soviet Union, and the other nuclear powers have analogous institutional structures.

These nuclear-driven institutional systems operate outside the public's consciousness much as do the ideological structures that provide the rationale for their existence. As George Kennan has pointed out, dismantling our war-preparedness apparatus would prove difficult even should the presumed basis for its existence—the enemy nation—disappear from the earth. More practical, perhaps, would be the diversion of the energies of war making to other problems, such as meeting the challenges of our eroding environment.

Our profound insecurity, our vulnerability and incapacity to protect ourselves from nuclear attack, have pressed political ideologies into bizarre, fear-driven extremes, especially in the United States. American anti-Sovietism, as theologian Harvey Cox has pointed out, has always contained religious elements (Cox, 1984; Dugger, 1984). But in the past few years anti-Sovietism, fear of nuclear annihilation, and Biblical literalism have been combined by a number of Protestant evangelical groups into an apocalyptic ideological system that unites hatred of the Soviet Union, a historical explanation of our present situation from Old and New Testament sources, and reassurances of salvation in the face of the nuclear threat through interpretations of these same scriptural texts.

The Reverend Jerry Falwell has been particularly successful among the present-day millennialists in structuring his prophecies of Armageddon in such a way as to satisfy simultaneously the political exigencies of power and the emotional needs of his congregation. In his telecast sermons, Falwell locates the source of evil and the nuclear threat in the Soviet Union, supports American militarism, and, like other Biblical fundamentalists, concocts his political history from Ezekiel, Jeremiah, Daniel, and Revelations. At the same time, however, he reassures his frightened followers that nuclear war, although the fulfillment of Biblical prophecy, will not come until *after* at least 1,007 years—1,000 to be spent with Jesus and 7 in the predicted "tribulation." Even then, when nuclear war—Armageddon—does come, the righteous will be saved and will rise up to join God in the "rapture." So, says Falwell, there is no need to worry about nuclear war. Through their apocalyptic religious ideologies and the focus on an outside evil enemy, present-day Christian millennialists seek to relieve their followers of the intense anxieties engendered by nuclear and other realities, which they, like all of us, find difficult to manage.

Discussion and Conclusions

Before concluding this chapter I will restate its central points. Most reasonable human beings know that by virtually any measure, nuclear weapons are failing to provide real security. On the contrary, there is a strong sense of powerlessness and fear of annihilation among citizens of the United States and other countries, most eloquently expressed by children and adolescents. Yet the nuclear nations continue to pile weapon upon weapon, threatening one another as if heedless of the ultimate consequences. The discoveries of a possible nuclear winter, a kind of final planetary catastrophe that could be caused by detonation of even a small fraction of the arsenals of the two superpowers, should have demonstrated once and for all the absurdity, futility, and danger of a continuing nuclear weapons spiral. But no turn toward reason and sanity has yet occurred, and it is doubtful that the nuclear winter findings have had any significant impact on the policies of the nuclear powers. These powers maintain their dangerous, militaristic, prenuclear habits as if oblivious to the radical changes in the nature of security necessitated by the properties of nuclear warheads and their continent-crossing delivery systems.

The problem is not, however, simply one of reason and rational argument. If it were, the education of the public and the leaders of the nuclear powers about these realities would be sufficient to change our homicidal/suicidal direction. There are, however, profound resistances to change, deeply ingrained collective habits, and emotional investments in continuing to do as we do, even if our eventual destruction must result. We are attached in particular to the habits of power and the economic rewards, domestic political advantage, career opportunities, and excitement and faith in technological progress which the nuclear system seems to provide. All these vested interests are embodied in institutional structures (private and public in the capitalist societies; principally public in the socialist countries), which provide the vehicle for delivering the system's rewards and organizational supports that make original, nonconformist thinking more difficult. Gratification of a wish for personal power, experienced most importantly through a kind of synergy between the individual and the nuclear state, offsets the powerlessness and loss of control that are the inescapable condition of individual human beings in the nuclear age.

Holding the whole international nuclear terror system together are the ideologies of East-West enmity. These collective thought structures justify and sustain the other emotional and material vested interests associated with the nuclear weapons competition. Without the fear, mistrust, and hatred which are simultaneously the stimuli and the by-products of polarizing ideologies, made more primitive by the regressive impact of nuclear terror, our commitment to perpetuating the arms race would collapse. As long as the ideological basis for the nuclear weapons competition goes unchallenged, neither we nor the Soviet Union seems willing to take responsibility for ending it.

National leaders have until now tended to define their responsibilities in the domain of international security largely in nationalistic terms. It is important that they (and all of us) come to view their responsibilities and personal identities more globally, consistent with the interdependence of the nuclear powers and the changed requirements of security in the nuclear age. One of the principal functions of ideology is to locate responsibility for a nation's problem elsewhere, preserving national self-esteem by maintaining an obliviousness to one's own nation's mass-murderous behaviors and proclivities. This collective psychological tendency in particular needs to be recognized, understood, and challenged.

In the United States we often hear the argument that we need nuclear weapons and nuclear strength to maintain our values of freedom, decency, and democracy. Yet these terms have become slogans used increasingly to justify the vested interests and the system of rewards that militarism and nuclearism yield. For the terror, secrecy, and corruption of our moral life that the addiction to nuclear war preparedness has brought about are gradually eroding the values they are intended to protect both at home and in other countries. Worse yet, the state of nuclear terror (Joel Kovel's term) may be contributing to an inability to tell the difference between the authentic meaning of freedom and democracy and the use of the words as Orwellian slogans behind which all manner of evil may be permitted.

The idea of a nuclear winter has become more than a description of the ecological disaster that would take place after the detonation of nuclear weapons. As Geiger has written, the nuclear winter is already here. It is a coldness of the human soul: "The nuclear winter that we endure now is a winter of the human spirit—a bleak, cold, contracted willingness to countenance destruction and self-destruction, pain and death, contamination and violence, ripping the web of life in a global madness. Nuclear winter is here. It is our very humanity that is freezing over" (1984, p. 12).

What I call for in this chapter, stimulated by the prospect of a nuclear winter, is a new kind of awareness, a recognition of how extensively nuclear war preparedness has affected our moral, spiritual, and institutional lives. We do not lack visions of a world that is free of the nuclear threat. Jonathan Schell, Freeman Dyson, and even Ronald Reagan in our time have offered inspiring possibilities, as did John Kennedy in 1963 and Dwight Eisenhower and Omar Bradley in the 1950s. But we have not taken adequate measure of the powerful forces that keep us attached to nuclear weapons, however much they may undermine our security.

Awareness alone will not solve the problem; it can only identify what we are up against in trying to treat our nuclear addiction. Knowledge, however, can help us plan strategies. In the United States it is to an informed citizenry that we need to look for change. Governments respond slowly to their people. But, they will, they must respond. William Slade, a former governor of Vermont, wrote almost 150 years ago of the power of citizen petition:

> The right of petition carries with it a tremendous power; for, though it wears the modest garb of a request, it really possesses by its moral influence, and by the consciousness of responsibility which it awakens in the representative body, the power almost of a command. The right of suffrage can be exercised but periodically—that of petition continually. It is a standing constitutional medium of communication from the people to their representatives. Its sacredness should be guarded, therefore, with the most wakeful jealousy; and it is thus guarded. . . . Woe, woe, to the representative who . . . treats it with contempt. (Stern, 1982, pp. 517–518)

Jerome B. Wiesner has said something similar in our own time:

Each citizen should realize that on the critical issues of what constitutes enough, what is an adequate deterrent, whether humanity can recover from a nuclear war, and many other such questions, his or her studied judgments are as good as those of a President or a Secretary of Defense. They may even be better, since he or she is not subjected to the pressures that impinge on people in official positions. (Wiesner, 1984)

Wiesner recommends that citizens form study groups to inform themselves about the facts and major issues in the nuclear weapons competition. Such a study group can then

build soundly based judgments about what is reasonable and what is exaggeration or untruth. At that state the group is in a position to fission, if that expression is permissible here, and begin new groups. This process can continue until there is a critical mass of citizens to help lead our leaders in a direction that will rescue us all. (Wiesner, 1984)

To overcome our heedless rush toward nuclear oblivion, we Americans will have to reclaim the control over our lives and security that we have surrendered to the nuclear strategists, perhaps believing—erroneously, as it has turned out—that as experts knowledgeable about the technical aspects of nuclear weapons and nuclear war they can be trusted with our security.

But if we in America change our ways, how do we know the Soviets would respond? After all, *we* live in a democracy, where citizen initiative makes a difference. But this argument is itself reflective of the ideologically grounded thinking that supports the nuclear arms race and the way it may insulate us from the reality of our own contribution to the problem. It may be true that Soviet citizens have less ability to influence their government's policies. But the argument also presumes that it is in the Soviet Union alone that the problem resides, or that the Soviets have a greater vested interest in maintaining the arms race than do we Americans. It overlooks Soviet initiatives, such as the ratification of the

SALT II accords and the renunciation of the first use of nuclear weapons, and the fact that it is the United States that
has led at virtually every step in the arms race. Without reviewing the arguments or justifications for our behavior, there
is no reason to assume that the Soviet Union would, in light
of the unparalleled suffering it experienced in the world wars
of the twentieth century and its profound realism about the
consequences of war, have a greater investment in maintaining the nuclear weapons competition than does the United
States. On the contrary, the greater relative economic drain
of the arms race on Soviet society and the less advanced
technological capability which forces the USSR always to play
catch up to American nuclear weapons progress might make
the Soviet Union *more* rather than less ready than the United
States to back away from the nuclear abyss.

Arthur F. Burns, U.S. ambassador to the Federal Republic of Germany, called in November 1984 for American initiatives that would lead to an improvement in the relationship between the United States and the Soviet Union. "It may
be," he said, "that significant progress on the crucial arms and
security issues can take place only as psychological attitudes
improve" (1984). We cannot know with certainty that Soviet
authorities will respond favorably to American initiatives
genuinely directed toward ending the threat of nuclear war.
But, as Ambassador Burns's words suggest, we have good
reason to believe that they would if the troubled emotional
climate that characterizes the relationship could be changed.
There is nothing to lose if we try. To go on as we are means
that eventually the bombs will be used and all we treasure on
this planet may come to an end. Sooner or later we will need
to recognize that American and Soviet security are interdependent. This is true not because we wish it to be so but because of the nature of nuclear weapons. There is no way that
we can achieve security unilaterally from a Soviet nuclear attack. We are utterly dependent on Russian forbearance.
Might not the kind of collaboration between the Soviet Union
and the United States that would be necessary to create the
conditions for genuine national and international security

eventually make the nuclear weapons themselves obsolete?
This seems a reasonable question with which to end the discussion.

References

American Catholic Bishops. (1982, October 26). Excerpts from
proposed letter on nuclear arms. *New York Times.*
Ash, T. G. (1984, November 22). Backyards: The U.S. case in
Central America. *New York Review of Books,* pp. 3–8.
Bachman, G. G. (1983). American high school seniors view the
military. *Armed Forces and Society, 10,* 86–104.
Beardslee, W. R., & Mack, J. E. (1982, spring). The impact on
children and adolescents of nuclear weapons. In *Psychosocial as-
pects of nuclear developments* (pp. 64–93). (Task Force Report No.
20, American Psychiatric Association).
Beardslee, W. R., & Mack, J. E. (1983). Adolescence and the
threat of nuclear war: The evolution of a perspective. *Yale Jour-
nal of Medicine, 56,* 79–91.
Bradley, O. N. (1957, November 5). This ultimate threat. Talk
given at a convocation at St. Albans School, Washington, DC.
Reprinted in *The New York Times,* April 10, 1981.
Bundy, M. (1984, March 23). Talk at luncheon. Avoiding Nuclear
War Project. Kennedy School of Government, Harvard Univer-
sity.
Burns, A. F. (1984, November 27). Reflections on East-West rela-
tions. Talk at a meeting of the Industrie Und Handelskammer.
Berlin, Germany.
Carey, M. J. (1983a). *Saying the unspeakable about the unthinkable.*
Unpublished manuscript.
Carey, M. J. (1983b). Letter to the author.
Chivian, E., & Goodman, J. (1984). What Soviet children are say-
ing about nuclear war. *International Physicians for the Prevention of
Nuclear War Report, 2*(1), 10–12.
Cox, H. (1984, October 2). Presentation at the Third Annual Esa-
len Institute Symposium on the Psychology of the U.S.–Soviet
Relationship, Big Sur, CA.
Dugger, R. (1984, April 8). Does Reagan expect a nuclear arma-
geddon? *The Washington Post.*
Editorial. (1984, February 24). *Science, 23*(4638), 775.
Eisenhower, D. (1956, April 4). Letter to Richard L. Simon, presi-

dent of Simon & Schuster. Reprinted in *The Washington Post,* September 7, 1983.

Erikson, E. (1969). *Gandhi's truth.* New York: Norton.

Erikson, E. (1985). Chapter in this book.

Frank, J. D. (1982, October). Pre-nuclear age leaders and the nuclear arms race. *American Journal of Ortho-Psychiatry, 52,* 632–637.

Frank, J. D. (1984, June 25). *Antinuclear admirals—an interview study.* Paper presented at the seventh annual meeting of the International Society of Political Psychology. Toronto, Ontario, Canada.

Geiger, H. J. (1984, October). The meaning of "nuclear winter": Scientific evidence and the human spirit. *International Physicians for the Prevention of Nuclear War Report, 2*(3), 8–12.

Goodman, L. A., Mack, J. E., Beardslee, W. R., & Snow, R. M. (1983). The threat of nuclear war and the nuclear arms race: Adolescent experience and perceptions. *Political Psychology, 4*(3), 501–530.

Kaplan, F. (1984, December 12). U.S. report sees a: "Nuclear winter." *The Boston Globe.*

Katz, J. (1985, January 5). Nuclear winter effects not settled. *The New York Times.*

Kennedy, J. F. (1963, June 10). Kennedy on the pursuit of peace in the nuclear age. Excerpts of a speech at American University, Washington, DC. Reprinted in *The Boston Globe,* November 22, 1983.

Kennen, G. (1984, September 24). Reflections: Two letters. *The New Yorker,* p. 55.

Kovel, J. (1983). *Against the state of nuclear terror.* Boston: South End Press.

Lawrence, A. W. (1963). Essay. In Liddell Hart, B. H., et al. (Eds.), *T. E. Lawrence by his friends* (pp. 145–151). New York: McGraw Hill.

Lebow, R. R. N., Jervis, R., & Gross Stein, J. (Eds.). (1985). Conclusions. In *Psychology and deterrence.* Baltimore: Johns Hopkins University Press.

Lewis, R. W. B. (1975). *Edith Wharton: A biography.* New York: Harper & Row.

Mack, J. E. (1983, November 21). Discussion at a Brookline community group, The Day Before. Brookline, MA.

Mack, J. E. (1984, August). Resistances to knowing in the nuclear age. *Harvard Educational Review, 54*(3), 260–270.

Mack, J. E. (1985). Toward a collective psychopathology of the nuclear arms race. *International Society of Political Psychology, 6.*

Oxford Research Group. (1984, June). Report prepared by Scilla McLean.

Peattie, L. (1984, March). Normalizing the unthinkable. *Bulletin of the Atomic Scientists, 40*(3), 32–36.

Pinderhughes, C. A. (1982). Paired differential bonding in biological, psychological and social systems. *American Journal of Social Psychiatry, 2*(3), 5–14.

Ramsey, N. (1984, November). Report prepared for the Oxford Research Group.

Rathjens, G. (1984, April 18). Discussion at the Avoiding Nuclear War Project. Kennedy School of Government, Harvard University.

Reagan, R. (1982, November 23). Address to nation on nuclear strategy toward the Soviet Union. *The New York Times.*

Reagan, R. (1983, March 24). Speech on military spending and a new defense. *The New York Times.*

Reagan, R. (1984, January 17). Speech on Soviet-American relations. *The New York Times.*

Reagan, R., & Mondale, W. (1984, October 22). Text of Reagan/Mondale answers at debate. *The Boston Globe.*

Sagan, C. (1983–1984, winter). Nuclear war and climatic catastrophe: Some policy implications. *Foreign Affairs, 62,* 257–292.

Schmookler, A. D. (1984). *The parable of the tribes: The problem of power in social evolution.* Berkeley: University of California Press.

Shaffer, H. (1983, October 1). Letter to the author.

Smith, L. (1983, October 11). Remarks at a workshop on public perceptions of nuclear weapons issues (organized by Dorothy S. Zinberg). Center for Science and International Affairs, John F. Kennedy School of Government, Harvard University.

Snow, R. M. (1984, March). Classroom discussion (videotaped). Boston English High School, Boston, MA.

Solantaus, T., Rimpela, M., & Taipale, Z. (1984). The threat of war in the minds of twelve-to-eighteen-year-olds in Finland. *Lancet, 8380*(1), 784.

Stern, H. J. (1982). Reconceiving the future. *Teacher's College Record, 84*(2), 509–519.

Stoddard, F., & Mack, J. E. (1985). Children, adolescents and the threat of nuclear war. In *Basic Handbook of Child Psychiatry* (Vol. 5).

Turco, R. P., Toon, O. B., Ackerman, T. P., Pollack, J. B., &

Sagan, C. (1983, December 23). Nuclear winter: Global consequences of multiple nuclear explosions. *Science, 222*(4630), 1283–1292.

Volkan, V. D. (1984, June 27). *The need to have enemies and allies: A developmental approach.* Based on presidential address presented at the seventh annual meeting of the International Society of Political Psychology, University College, Toronto, Canada.

Vonnegut, K. (1983, December 31). Weapons junkies: The worst addiction of them all. *The Nation.*

Wiesner, J. B. (1984, October 7). A perilous sense of security. *The Boston Globe Magazine,* p. 10.

Yankelovich, D., & Doble, J. (1984, fall). The public mood: Nuclear weapons and the U.S.S.R. *Foreign Affairs, 63,* 33–46.

York, H. (1970). *Race to oblivion.* New York: Simon & Schuster.

Zuckerman, E. (1984, November 25). The-end-of-the-world scenarios. *The New York Times.*

Unexamined Assumptions and Inescapable Consequences

HENRY STEELE COMMAGER

The fundamental problems of politics, in the modern as in the ancient world, are moral. To the ancients the maxim that no state could long flourish without virtue was clear; equally clear was—and is—the conclusion that no state has ever conducted itself virtuously over a long span of years. The philosophical and practical debate over this problem has agitated statesmen and philosophers from the beginnings of history. Most familiar is Thucydides' unembellished account of the debate over the fate of the people of Melos; he left his readers to draw their own conclusions about this earliest recorded exercise of "Reason of State." All, too, are familiar with the New Testament account of Herod's Massacre of the Innocents—an episode which again conjured up reasons of state.

That issue is very much with us today, with greater urgency than at any previous era of history. Now, with the recognition of the nuclear winter, it is for the first time one that directly concerns not just one people or one nation but the whole of mankind. It is one that, historically and philosophically, American experience illuminates.

From the beginning of their independent history, Americans assumed that they could somehow escape the fate that history had meted out to other peoples. Protected as they were by a wide ocean, aloof from the quarrels which, as Jefferson wrote, had afflicted nations "who feel power and forget right," and blessed "with land enough for our descendants to the thousandth and thousandth generation," they believed that they might confound the history of the past and advance to "destinies beyond the reach of mortal eye."

Most Americans (not dour old John Adams, to be sure) persuaded themselves that they could indeed. Thus, Tom Paine asserted that the American "was a new Adam in a new paradise." So, too, the "Poet of the Revolution," Philip Freneau, boasted that

Paradise anew shall flourish
By no second Adam lost.

And, more elaborately, Washington's favorite poet, David Humphreys, wrote that

All former empires rose, the work of guilt,
On conquest, blood, or usurpation built
But we, taught wisdom by their woes and crimes
Fraught with their lore, and born in better times
Our constitutions form'd on freedom's base, *-etc. ad
infinitum*

In his First Inaugural Address, Washington made it official:

The foundation of our national policy will be laid in the pure and immutable principles of private morality. . . . [For] there is no truth more thoroughly established than that there exists in the economy and course of nature an indissoluble union between virtue and happiness, between duty and advantage, between the genuine maxims of an honest and magnanimous policy and the solid rewards of public prosperity and felicity.

Though there were antecedents in the ancient and even in the early modern world, it was Machiavelli who first used the concept of Reason of State in the sense in which it has since been accepted and who first propounded the arguments that have ever since been used to vindicate it. With his writings—*The Prince, Discourses on Livy,* and *History of Florence*—he gave it not only dignity and authority but almost official status. Machiavelli's concern was not with morals but with power. His philosophy was secular, his logic that embraced by most modern nations: the claims of the state take precedence over all competing claims; and the survival, prosperity, and glory of the state are the ultimate good. It was a logic embraced alike by princes and aristocracies, and, in modern times, by republican-democratic and communist-totalitarian states.

Quite rightly, by his own logic, Machiavelli did not regard himself as an enemy of morality. That logic was merely a secularization of religious philosophy. For some centuries religion had taught that the triumph of the true Church justified any conduct, including mass exile, torture, or war. The Church had presided readily enough over the Massacre of St. Bartholomew's Eve, and Voltaire, who devoted much of his life to *écrasez l'infame*, was damned by the Church for *his* infamy.

Machiavelli addressed himself to the prosperity and glory of Florence—and of Italy. That goal was, he held, a moral one: the triumph of the House of Medici and the absorption of rival states and cities alone would ensure peace, prosperity, and power to Italy. It followed, therefore, that whatever contributed to that end was moral, whatever weakened its attainment immoral. The Prince, then, must be prepared to exercise power, even ultimate power, for the good of Florence and of Italy. To achieve this he must have absolute authority over his subjects so that he might force them to be virtuous and punish them if they rejected virtue.[1]

Machiavelli did not know it, but he prepared the way for the ultimate victory of political, military, and economic nationalism, each of which was, in turn, prepared to formulate its own version of ethics if essential to its triumph:

> So our unfortunate country supplicates heaven to
> raise up a prince who may free her from the odious and
> humiliating yoke of foreigners . . . who may close the
> numberless wounds with which she has been so long af-
> flicted and under whose standard she may march against
> her cruel oppressors. . . . Every war that is necessary is
> just. (Machiavelli, *The Prince*)

1. How that principle flourished! Two centuries later, Charles Frederick of Baden proclaimed his determination to make all his "subjects free, opulent, and law-abiding citizens whether they liked it or not."

Few chapters in the history of civilization are more instructive than that which recounts the emergence in the eighteenth century of modern nationalism and modern science and the hope that the Enlightenment, associated with science, would make good its claim to be exempt from exploitation. That chapter is particularly interesting to us because it was in the New World and under the auspices of Thomas Jefferson and his associates that that goal was realized. It was, alas, a brief interlude, for modern nationalism quickly rejected such concepts as morality, virtue, and ethics in favor of the claims of nationalism—as it still does!

Yet, during much of the eighteenth century and well into the nineteenth, the standard-bearers of the Enlightenment in the Old and New Worlds alike were able to assume the preeminence of the claims of science over those of politics. "Everywhere," as historian Friedrich Meinecke says, "they introduced a joyous forward impulse." Thus, David Hume championed an international, not a national, commerce and "prayed for the commerce of Germany, Spain, Italy and even France." Thus Joseph Banks, for forty-two years president of the Royal Society, was sponsor and guardian of science everywhere: it was he who persuaded George III to turn over a rich collection of plants captured from a French ship to the *Jardin de Roi*, over which that other philosophe, the Comte de Buffon, presided. Thus, the radical Dr. Priestley, beloved of Jefferson, championed first the American and then the French revolutions; and when a Birmingham mob destroyed his library and his scientific laboratory he found refuge in America. On Priestley's arrival in New York, the mayor sailed out to welcome him, churchbells rang, and cannons saluted. Three states invited him to take up residence, and two universities offered him chairs of chemistry and of philosophy, while Mr. Jefferson invoked Priestley's aid for his projected university. That is not the way we greet revolutionaries today. In France, too, the philosophes formed a powerful intellectual society—a society committed to cosmopolitanism, peace, and the universal authority of *natural*—that is, scientific—philosophy. In Germany Lessing, Haller, Kant, and, above all, Goethe considered themselves cosmopolites, not

Germans. Alas, their numbers grew fewer and fewer with the triumph of nationalism.

Clearly, in the eyes of the natural philosophers there was no incompatability between science and humanism or between cosmopolitanism and nationalism: their philosophy and their vision encompassed both. And what a vision it was! Except in the realm of science there has been nothing like it since.

It was an age when the United States, speaking through Dr. Franklin, and France, through Jacques Necker, decreed immunity for Captain Cook's ships, which were engaged in the exploration of the Pacific, because Cook and his crew were "the common friends of mankind." It was an age when Rousseau could pay tribute to "those great cosmopolitan minds that make light of the barriers that sunder nation from nation, and embrace all mankind within their benevolence." It was an age when George III could retain the American Benjamin West as court artist and when—all through the Revolutionary War—West could welcome American students to his atelier. It was a day when, at the request of Joseph Banks, Napoleon could intervene to free the scientist Dolomieu from imprisonment in a Naples dungeon and, a few years later, at the height of the war between France and the Germanies, grant immunity to the university city of Göttingen because it boasted in Christian Heyne the greatest classical scholar of the age. It was in 1800, too, that the French *institut* could confer its gold medal on Sir Humphrey Davy and, while the war still raged, Davy could cross the Channel to accept the medal, to the plaudits of his fellow scientists. "Some people," wrote Sir Humphrey, "say I ought not to accept this prize, but if the two governments are at war, the men of science are not." That note resounded all through the Enlightenment, even in its twilight. It was Dr. Jenner of smallpox fame who put it most succinctly. "The scientists," he said, "are never at war. Peace must always preside in those bosoms whose object is the augmentation of human happiness."

A century and a half later, Albert Einstein made the same point more concisely: "Politics are for the moment, an equation is for eternity."

Much of this was the expression of individuals. Much of it, too, was an expression of enlightened academic and governmental policies. How illuminating is the history of the Royal Society, founded in 1642 by Charles II under the auspices of such "natural" and "moral" philosophers as Sir Isaac Newton and John Locke, and embracing in its membership men of letters as well as men of science. It was Christopher Wren, professor of astronomy at Oxford University and architect of St. Paul's Cathedral, who drafted the charter:

> The way to so happy a government . . . is in no manner more facilitated than by the promoting of useful arts which . . . are found to be the basis of civil communities and free government, and which gather multitudes, *by an orpheus charm*, into cities and companies. . . . [The society, therefore, was to] meet weekly and confer about the hidden causes of things, with a design . . . to prove themselves real benefactors to mankind.

A century later the American Philosophical Society wrote a similar provision into its charter: "Whereas nations truly civilized will never wage war with the arts and sciences, and the common interests of mankind, the Society should retain cordial relations with Learned Societies everywhere in the world, regardless of politics and war."

Some of the Enlightenment philosophers had already gone so far as to propose learned academies not merely to advance knowledge but to guide the destinies of nations. That was the essence of Condorcet's ambitious plan in *The New Atlantis*, which proposed an international society of natural philosophers whose members would be concerned not so much with practical investigations as with pure research. It was to be sponsored by crowned heads of nations and supported by contributions from several governments, the aristocracy, and, prophetically enough, by "the business and commercial community." "All the scientists," Condorcet asserted, would "be animated by a passion for truth," and governments eager to contribute "to the happiness of the human species" would follow the society's recommendations.

Poor Condorcet, with all his hopes, died by his own hand in order to escape the guillotine.

The philosophy that animated Lessing and Turgot and Condorcet was the Platonic concept of a republic where Kings would be Philosophers and Philosophers, Kings. That did not work out—except in America. There, alone, it was the philosophers, natural and moral alike, who were in fact chosen by the people to guide the affairs of state: Benjamin Franklin, Thomas Jefferson, James Madison, John Jay, John Adams, who drafted the Constitution of Massachusetts, with its special provisions for Harvard College and for the arts and the sciences, and founded the American Academy of Arts and Sciences, and his son John Quincy Adams, the founder of the Smithsonian Institution.

The superiority of the claims of science and philosophy over those of the state was as much a part of the American revolutionary tradition as the principle of the supremacy of the civil over the military. That principle was never more felicitously put than by the then governor Jefferson in his letter to young David Rittenhouse in 1778:

> Your time for two years past has been principally employed in the civil government of your country. Tho' I have been aware of the authority our cause would acquire from it being known that yourself and Dr. Franklin were zealous friends to it, and am myself duly impressed with a sense of the arduousness of government, and the obligation those are under who are able to conduct it; yet I am also satisfied that there is an order of geniuses above that obligation and therefore exempt from it. Nobody can conceive that nature ever intended to throw away a Newton upon the occupations of a crown: it would have been a prodigality for which even providence might have been arraigned, had he been by birth annexed to what was so far beneath him.

Goethe, greatest of the German cosmopolites, had predicted that "Science and Art belong to the whole world, and the barriers of nationality vanish before them." That proved a rash prediction, especially for a philosopher whose life overlapped those of both Frederick the Great and Bismarck. For from the historian's point of view it is neither Hume nor Adam Smith, Jefferson nor Hamilton who are the most illuminating characters, but Frederick the Great himself and after him Hegel. Both contributed to the Enlightenment: both formulated, acted on, and rationalized Reason of State; both went back to Machiavelli to provide a secular rather than a theological rationalization for their concepts; and both inspired disciples in the academy and on the battlefields of power.

Frederick thought of himself as "enlightened," and in this he had the support of no other than Voltaire. Had he not abolished torture? Had he not permitted a limited freedom of the press? Was he not something of a musician, something of a poet, something even of a philosophe? What is more, he had written a *Political Testament* setting forth with compelling logic the philosophy of the Enlightenment and, then, to vindicate his credentials, wrote another treatise he called *Anti-Machiavelli*.

All this was a manifestation of the paradox of his career. In his determination to exalt Prussia and to enlarge its territories, he outdid all his contemporaries in lawlessness, treachery, and deceit. He marched his armies into Silesia and Bohemia, waged war off and on for twenty years, and made, and broke, treaties as suited his interests or his conceit. Perhaps Goethe had him in mind when he wrote that "whoever *acts*, is always unscrupulous."

Whether Frederick was the inspiration and the model for later German exercises of Reason of State or whether that philosophy was particularly suited to the problem of unifying some two hundred tiny principalities into a nation eludes both historians and philosophers. The first sustained rationalization of his policies came from Johann Gottlieb Fichte, who assured his countrymen that they were a "primordial nation" and one "in which the growth of human perfection is most decisively present." "If you perish," he admonished them, "the whole of mankind will perish." He was, too, one of the first to preach racial purity and to argue that the Germans alone had a "unique superior life and were selected by the deity to preserve it and spread it."

Fichte's contemporary Georg Hegel was even more deeply obsessed with the notion of Nordic superiority and of the destiny of the German people to rule the world. With him, Machiavellianism came to form an integral part in a complex which, at the same time, embraced all political and all moral values; and with him moral values were all but identical with German values. "Truth," he argued, "resides in power," and he wanted power to reside in Germany!

The philosophy of Reason of State stretches from Machiavelli to Frederick the Great to Fichte and Hegel, and from them to Bismarck and Von Moltke, who asserted that "eternal peace is but a dream, and not a beautiful dream. War is part of God's Cosmic Order: without wars, the world would sink into materialism." All this, in turn, led to the reductio ad absurdum: Nietzsche's aphorism "You say it is a good cause which hallows every war. I say it is the good war which hallows every cause." From here the road to Hitler is direct.

The drama of morality in America was to be played out against these two competing, or alternating, backgrounds: the background of nationalism (we were, after all, the first nation to be "made") and the background of modern science. The animating drive of the first was the wealth and glory of the state; the animating impulse of the second, enlightenment and cosmopolitanism. The seminal principle of the first was power; that of the second, "the illimitable freedom of the human mind."

Americans have never been willing formally to acknowledge the principle of Reason of State. Here, as elsewhere, they have preferred to find more exalted arguments for justifying their conduct: that they are "God's Children" or "His Chosen People," or that their country is the "Promised Land" and their government the "Last Best Hope of Earth." These are not only euphemisms but substitutes for reason; and however nature and history may have conspired to provide supporting evidence for these terms, the rationale has commonly been that which animated all other modern states.

The American version of Reason of State was, from the beginning, based on religion and culture. These combined speedily to conjure up the conceit of "Manifest Destiny"—a destiny more manifest to the Americans who profited from it than to the native inhabitants who were its victims. The philosophy of Manifest Destiny was not in fact very different from that elaborated by Machiavelli: first, that God had presided over the migration from the Old World to the New; second, that God could not have intended that so vast and rich a territory should be confined to a few scattered tribes, but looked with favor on its occupation by an enlightened Christian people.[2] (The native peoples were after all heathens and, unless prepared to be converted, were destined for eternal damnation.)

This philosophy had the immense advantage that it could not be refuted and could be refurbished for almost any new circumstance. It justified "Indian Removal"—a policy that continued until all the native peoples were removed to reservations, assimilated, or killed. It applied to the territories controlled by Spanish peoples as well as by Indians, thus justifying the annexation of the two Floridas and the military acquisition of Texas and California and all the land between: if the Spaniards and Mexicans were not heathens, they were Catholics, and that was almost as bad. It rationalized—and still does—American hegemony over the Caribbean and then, with less logic, over Hawaii and the Philippines, and eventually the Pacific.

Manifest Destiny could be stretched, if necessary, to justify slavery as well as conquest. Thus generations of civilized and virtuous Christians persuaded themselves that slavery, far from being a "necessary evil," was a positive good—a blessing to slaves and masters alike. We should take this long and painful chapter of our history to heart, for better than anything else in our experience it makes clear how a civilized

2. This was precisely the theme of that monstrous epic poem of four thousand rhymed couplets, *The Vision of Columbus,* by that poet-manqué Joel Barlow.

nation could persist for two hundred years in practicing and justifying what the world now recognizes as immoral.

Some features of this American Reason of State persisted long after formal slavery was a thing of the past and manifestations of racial prejudice were outlawed by constitutional amendment. Prejudice persisted and emerged thirty years after the Civil War, when, as the *Washington Post* put it: "The taste of empire is in the mouth of the people even as the taste of blood is in the jungle. It means an imperial policy, the Republic renascent, taking her place with the armed nations."

It was this imperial policy that dictated the three-year war against the Filipinos, fighting for their independence. It was a war characterized by moral arrogance, the illusion of the "White Man's Burden," and brutality. Reason of State here was a curious amalgam of imperialism, commercial interest, and religion, all bundled together in President McKinley's famous explanation of how God directed him to "civilize and Christianize" the Philippines.

The same rationalization of prejudices, interests, and moral arrogance emerges in our own day. It was evident in the "relocation" during World War II of over 100,000 Japanese— most of them American citizens—and again in the Vietnam War. Now that that desperate chapter of our history is behind us (so, at least, we delude ourselves), we take what comfort we can from the spectacle of the Russians in Afghanistan or the South Africans in Namibia. But history will remember, even as we are busy forgetting, that the war in Vietnam was against a people ten thousand miles distant, with whom we had no quarrel and who did not, and could not, threaten us; and that in the course of that war we rained 7 million tons of bombs on a country the size of New Mexico— three times the tonnage we dropped on Germany and Japan during World War II.

It is scarcely necessary to illustrate the American propensity for justification by Reason of State in what is surely the most fateful series of decisions made in recorded history: the decision to drop the bomb on Hiroshima and Nagasaki in August 1945 and the decision (also by Truman) to go ahead with the hydrogen bomb in 1953. Neither the military nor the larger international justifications that have been proffered will, I think, be accepted by later generations. But how revealing, in this connection, that many Americans have already put out of their minds, and their consciences, responsibility for inaugurating the Age of Atomic Warfare. Indeed, by a process of self-induced amnesia, they still talk of the threat of a first strike and how such a strike is to be prevented, just as if we had not already made the first strike almost forty years ago, and at a time when there was no danger of a counterstrike that we had to "deter."

As we contemplate this long record, we may still conclude that we are indeed God's Chosen People, but only if we believe William Cowper's assurance that "God moves in a mysterious way, his wonders to perform."

It is interesting that the term *Reason of State* was not coined by Machiavelli himself but by the Archbishop Giovanni della Casa, in connection with a controversy between church and empire some years after the great Florentine's death. There are, the archbishop observed prophetically, two kinds of Reasons of State, one "false and unbridled, and good for any infamy," the other "honorable and steadfast, such as those observed in courts of law." The latter; he concluded, was the one to be followed.

That had been taken for granted by Machiavelli and by his many successors pretty much down to our own day, and the distinction was easy to make: the "false and unbridled" Reasons of State were those flaunted by one's enemies, the "honorable and steadfast" were those that one observed. From the expulsion of the Moors and Jews from Spain to the Holocaust in Germany, from the enslavement of Africans in America to the devastation of Vietnam, Reason of State dictated the policies—and vindicated them. And in every case that rationalization was moral as well as political, for in every case the preservation and exaltation of the state has been the supreme virtue; and, in almost every case, it has been a virtue hallowed by religion, or itself a religion. Just as in the

Age of the Crusades, of the Religious Wars, and the Conquest of the New World, religion authorized imposing the true Gospel on those otherwise doomed to damnation, so in the modern world the religions of fascism, of Nazism, of communism, and even of democracy have also justified subversion, force, and conquest.

If we find it hard to believe that any civilized people could rationalize the extermination of all the males on the island of Melos, the Massacre of the Innocents, the expulsion of the Huguenots from France, the persecution of Catholics in Ireland, the killings of millions of Moslems and Hindus in India, the extermination of Jews in Germany, let us reflect that millions of blacks today doubtless find it hard to understand how civilized peoples could not only rationalize slavery and the slave trade as a blessing but—in the end—fight four years for its preservation.

That eminent student of the history of nationalism Hans Morgenthau concludes his *Pathology of Politics* with the reflection that moralizing about politics or international relations has never produced any significant results, but adds, somewhat lamely, that "nonetheless, morals may have a considerable impact on politics." Those who sit in the seats of power, however—a Stalin who asked "How many battalions has the Pope?," a Hitler who tried to exterminate all Jews, an American general who urged that we "bomb Vietnam back to the Stone Age," a CIA which unblushingly acknowledged a dozen attempts to assassinate Fidel Castro—are inclined to dismiss those who object to all these improprieties as, in Hegel's words, "trivial moralists." Even former Secretary of State Kissinger, who would never for a moment condone the iniquities of a Hitler, when confronted by Vietnamese intransigence about signing a final agreement to cease fire, could observe that "a week's bombing would have put this agreement in perspective."

Nationalism breeds and encourages not only a double standard of morality but, what is even more deeply rooted, paranoia about potential enemies. It is not only those familiar with Latin who know that *hostis* means both enemy and stranger. In a more innocent era, Americans achieved a modification of this: because most Americans came here as strangers and because in many a frontier society the stranger was the bearer of news, "stranger" came to be a term of welcome, and even today enlightened communities have a "welcome wagon" for newcomers. With the rise of the city, the influx of immigrants from southern and eastern Europe and of blacks from the South, the word reassumed some of its traditional connotations. And, as the United States became a world power, it became increasingly easy to regard nations that were not "with us" as "against us."

In his Farewell Address, Washington could warn us most solemnly against "inveterate antipathies against particular nations," but in the past fifty years we have applied the word *enemy* to half the human race. This is national paranoia on a scale almost unprecedented in history. We are familiar with the consequences of religious paranoia from the days of the Crusades to the current wars and persecutions that rage in every quarter of the globe, except perhaps our own. In the past, nationalist paranoia—that of the French and the Germans about each other, the Italians and the Austrians, the Turks and the Greeks, the smoldering Irish hostility to England, the hostility of the slaveholding states to the free states of the Union—could be localized. Now not only are animosities global but the weapons that science and technology have provided to indulge them are global in their impact. Atomic radiation and nuclear winter respect neither political nor geographical boundaries but threaten the end of the earth.

Confronted with a situation that seemed desperate, theologian Reinhold Niebuhr found some consolation in the faith that "the instinct for survival involved in all these manifestations of egoism is true for nations as for individuals." That instinct survives in individuals. But our government has lost it or betrayed it.

We delude ourselves that it is possible for us to survive in a world where all our rivals and enemies go under. It is on this fallacious assumption that we have built our "security"

for the past forty years—the assumption of "winning" a nuclear arms race. That race has gone on now for nearly a half
century, and victory is more distant today than it was when
we inaugurated it with the atomic bomb and accelerated it
with the hydrogen bomb. Against all evidence and against
common sense we persisted in it, assuming—again in the face
of compelling evidence to the contrary—that we could somehow both outspend and outsmart those we chose to regard
as "enemies." For twenty years one of those "enemies" was
China: did not Dean Rusk warn us that a "million Chinese
might land on the shores of California"? Mysteriously, almost absentmindedly, we got over our paranoia about China
and discovered instead that it was a friend, a trading part-
ner, and, just possibly, an ally. But our paranoia about the
Soviet Union feeds upon itself ever more voraciously.

Why do we suppose, against all experience, that we can
dissuade the Russians from holding their own in weapons
production? Clearly, Russian scientists can do anything we can
do; clearly, too, a totalitarian government is in a better position to impose its will on its people, and on industry, technology, and scientific research.

More persuasive—certainly to men of reason and good
will—is the knowledge that a nuclear war will be suicidal not
only for both contestants but, in all likelihood, for the human race. Even if there should be some survivors from nuclear fire and nuclear winter, their familiar world—including
all those objectives for which we now contend—would be gone
forever.

Why, then, do we persist in a military solution (the very
term is an oxymoron) instead of seeking in good faith a diplomatic, political, economic, and moral solution? Why, with
the sunlight of two hundred years of progress and security
shining upon us, do our leaders turn away from our long record of seeking peace and progress through science and
technology, or of following our tradition of magnanimity in
the conduct of foreign policy? Why have we turned away from
Newton and Locke, with their reliance on Reason, to the
desperate philosophy of Thomas Hobbes, who exalted only

Reason of State as interpreted by the reasoning of kings?

This dramatic shift from the philosophy which presided over the Enlightenment to that which presided over totalitarianism is already moving like a dark cloud over our political and moral horizon. The author of *The Leviathan* relied on deductive, not inductive, reasoning. His dogmas were absolute: the absolute insignificance of the common man and the absolute glory of the king; the absolute danger of popular interference with the affairs of government and the absolute wisdom of those who crowded about the throne; the conviction that power, too, must be absolute and must be lodged neither in the people nor in magistrates but in the ruler alone; a ready acceptance of "force and fraud" as legitimate in national or international relations—indeed, as Hobbes wrote, "Force and Fraud in war are the cardinal virtues," just as, we might add, the principle that animates the CIA.

As President Pouncey of Amherst College recently observed, we live in a society "precariously balanced between good and evil, restraint and aggression, generosity and selfishness, but we live in a period of history, indeed in a moment when, for the first time, the tilting of these balances, one way or another, can have a cosmic consequence."

Opposing the Nuclear Threat: The Convergence of Moral Analysis and Empirical Data

J. BRYAN HEHIR

This chapter will examine the concept of nuclear winter from the perspective of religious and moral values. The objective is to identify points of intersection between the empirical arguments about nuclear winter and ethical perspectives on nuclear war. The analysis will move through three steps: (1) the context of the nuclear debate; (2) the ethical and empirical contributions to the nuclear debate; and (3) implications for policy drawn from the ethical-empirical data.

The Context of the Nuclear Debate

The scientific studies about the possibility of a nuclear winter have been among the most startling contributions to the nuclear debate of the 1980s. These studies fit, however, within a broader framework of public discussion that preceded the nuclear winter predictions and will determine in part the long-term impact of the nuclear winter information on the public mind. It was this broader public debate that the National Conference of Catholic Bishops described in 1983 as a "new moment" in the nuclear age (pp. 40 ff.). The moment is new because the character of the nuclear debate in the 1980s is strikingly different from the debate of the previous two decades. The shift in the public argument can be analyzed at two levels: the "popular," or citizens' debate and the "policy," or specialists' debate. At both levels there is something new in the 1980s, and both have been affected by the discussion of the nuclear winter.

At the popular level there has emerged a broad-based coalition of citizens in the United States who are determined to share in and shape the nuclear policy of the nation. The representatives of this popular coalition include the freeze movement, the physicians, and the religious community. The policy proposals of these three groups are not always identical, and they do not exhaust the spectrum of the popular involvement. Nevertheless, the impact of citizen engagement in the nuclear question has amounted to a democratization of the policy debate. The discussion of what U.S. nuclear policy should be is no longer confined to the halls of government and policy institutes of universities. In the 1980s the nuclear debate in the United States is pursued in church halls, public libraries, and on prime-time television. The consequences of this newfound public interest are registered in a fascinating article by pollster Daniel Yankelovitch in *Foreign Affairs* (1984). His review of the polling data records a major shift in American public opinion on the nuclear question. Between the 1950s and the 1980s a significant majority of the American public moved from the view that nuclear weapons enhanced American security to the position that new weapons in either American or Soviet hands are a threat to our security.

The "new moment" is not only a product of a shift in citizen attitudes. A critically important complement to this popular change has been a recasting of specialized policy debate. Within a policy framework that for most of the nuclear age had been remarkably consensual, a new degree of pluralism emerged in the 1980s. The nuclear debate at the policy level had always manifested strongly held differences of view on specific questions, but the core premises of the policy seemed untouchable. The pluralism of the 1980s included dissent from the core consensus by people who had helped shape the received doctrine. The issue that symbolized this elite dissent most clearly was a *Foreign Affairs* article by McGeorge Bundy, George Kennan, Robert McNamara, and Gerard Smith advocating a "no first use" declaration by NATO (1982). The proposal contradicted NATO doctrine that had been stable for thirty-eight years, and its authors represented the founding fathers of the strategy of the Western alliance. The full range of the pluralism in the nuclear debate can be understood only in light of President Reagan's proposal for a strategic defense initiative (SDI); this was dissent from within

the policy process at the highest level. The SDI proposal was
at least as much of a challenge to the doctrine of deterrence
as the freeze proposal. As appealing as the notion of "defense" against nuclear attack sounds at first hearing, it still
must be recognized that the idea stands foursquare against
what deterrence has come to mean in the nuclear age. One
need not be highly enthusiastic about deterrence to continue
to have grave reservations about trying to solve our deterrence dilemma by moving to defense.

Between the freeze on the one hand and the SDI on the
other stands a third example of the pluralism of the policy
debate in the 1980s. It is the Scowcroft Report, the report
of a commission convoked by the president to analyze the
status of U.S. nuclear forces in light of the proposal to deploy the MX missile. The commission was drawn from the
center-right of the political spectrum, and its primary purpose was to convince the Congress of the value of the MX
missile. The Scowcroft Report did conclude that the United
States needed the MX, but the premises of the report (that a
window of vulnerability does *not* exist and that multiwarhead
land-based missiles are not a wise course to pursue) provided
critics of the MX with some of their best arguments against
it. The report illustrated the inner tensions of the U.S. strategic debate in the 1980s.

The convergence of this pluralistic policy debate and the
upsurge of public interest produced a situation in which
consensus on American nuclear strategy could no longer be
presumed in the general public or among policy elites. By
the mid-1980s it was clear that the very concept of deterrence was under attack from the Left and the Right of the
American political system. The "new moment" is an open
moment in which the nuclear debate is being pressed to its
ultimate foundations. It is easier to criticize deterrence than
to create an alternative, and most of the critics recognize this
sobering fact. But the presumption that deterrence has
"worked" for forty years and that this should mean it will work
for twoscore more is not widely held. One need not dispar-

age deterrence in order to agree with the Catholic bishops' judgment that "we cannot consider it adequate as a long-term basis for peace" (National Conference, 1983, p. 58).

The nuclear winter data fit into this broader horizon of profound doubt about the wisdom, morality, and viability of nuclear deterrence. How this new scientific information fits into the wider policy debate is my next concern.

Ethical and Empirical Contributions to the Policy Debate

One of the most interesting features of the "new moment" in the nuclear debate is the relationship of ethical and empirical arguments. For most of the nuclear age the public and policy debates have been dominated by hard data, quantifiable characteristics that measure "throw weight," missile accuracy, deployment and targeting strategies, and levels of armaments. Soft data (intangibles) have never been wholly absent from the debate since deterrence has been as dependent upon psychological characteristics as upon the physical capacities of missile systems. Similarly, the alliance system of NATO has been as dependent upon trust as upon the numbers of missiles stationed in Europe. But the status of soft data in the policy debate has always been uncertain, and ethical or moral considerations are clearly soft data. The debate of the 1980s has been strikingly different because of the enhanced role given to soft data. The public interpretation given to the dilemma of the nuclear age reaches beyond the number of missiles to more human and humane considerations. Today citizens and specialists alike are more likely to stress the nonempirical elements of the nuclear dilemma than were the debates of the past twenty-five years.

It is not surprising that in this context the role of moral argument has taken on new visibility in the nuclear debate. The 1980s have produced a new *interest* in the moral dimensions of the nuclear question and a new level of *analysis* of the moral issues.

The Catholic bishops' pastoral letter, *The Challenge of Peace*, is one example of how the moral argument about nuclear strategy has entered the public debate. The pastoral letter itself contains an extensive mix of ethical and empirical arguments. In this section, I will summarize its central moral judgments and then examine areas of convergence with the nuclear winter position.

The basic objective of the pastoral letter is to build a barrier against the use of nuclear weapons. This objective is based in part on a judgment that pervades the entire letter and that makes a qualitative distinction between nuclear weapons and other forms of weaponry. Precisely because the destructive capacity of nuclear war is so overwhelming and the chances of controlling nuclear weapons are so fragile and few, the bishops argued that the empirical distinction between nuclear and conventional weapons should also be seen as a moral distinction. The moral arguments and policy recommendations of the pastoral letter are designed to construct a political, strategic, psychological, and moral barrier against resort to the use of any nuclear weapons.

This basic objective of the pastoral letter is supported by a series of specific judgments about the use of nuclear weapons and about deterrence policy.

The letter comments on three cases of use of nuclear weapons. The first case is that of directly intended attacks on civilian populations, or "Counter-Population Warfare," which is considered for two reasons: (1) the moral principle at stake, noncombatant immunity, is central to the just-war ethic, and (2) at various times in the nuclear age the direct targeting of civilian centers has been considered or planned. The pastoral letter's analysis contains three significant characteristics. First, the basic judgment of the letter is to rule out, absolutely, direct attacks on civilian populations. Second, the judgment is based upon the just-war tradition, which found forceful expression in the Second Vatican Council's statement against "destruction of entire cities or of extensive areas along with their population. . . . It merits unequivocal and unhesitating condemnation" (Vatican II, 1976). Third, the American bishops provide an application of this principle with direct relevance for nuclear strategy: they rule out retaliatory action against civilian populations even if our cities have been hit first.

The second case, "The Initiation of Nuclear War," is the question of first use of nuclear weapons. The significance of this issue is twofold; the possibility of first use is still a central piece of NATO strategy, and a renewed debate about the strategy is now underway (see Bundy et al. 1982; Kaiser et al., 1982). The bishops do not address the political debate as such; their purpose is to isolate the moral question in it. Briefly stated, is there a specific moral issue involved in the willingness to be the first party to move warfare from the conventional level to the nuclear level?

The pastoral letter finds a specific moral responsibility here, and its judgment is one of the more controversial sections of the letter. The bishops say: "We do not perceive any situation in which deliberate initiation of nuclear warfare, on however restricted a scale, can be morally justified. Non-nuclear attacks by another state must be resisted by other than nuclear means. Therefore, a serious moral obligation exists to develop non-nuclear defensive strategies as rapidly as possible" (National Conference, 1983, p. 47).

The third case is "Limited Nuclear War." Here again, the bishops enter a much disputed technical question with a long history. They are aware that they cannot settle the empirical debate of whether a limited nuclear exchange can be kept limited. Their approach in the pastoral letter is to raise a series of questions that express their radical skepticism about controlling such an exchange. Having pressed the question of what *limited* really means, they make the following assessment: "One of the criteria of the just-war tradition is a reasonable hope of success in bringing about justice and peace. We must ask whether such a reasonable hope can exist once nuclear weapons have been exchanged. The burden of proof remains on those who assert that meaningful limitation is possible" (National Conference, 1983, p. 50).

Since the dominant thrust of the pastoral letter is to prevent any use of nuclear weapons, its specific prohibitions against first use and the extreme skepticism of the bishops about the notion of limiting the damage in a nuclear exchange are not surprising. In light of this severe critique of use, the bishops move to a moral analysis of deterrence. After an extensive discussion of the empirical elements of deterrence policy and a review of recent Catholic teaching on deterrence, they make their judgment about U.S. deterrence policy: "These considerations of concrete elements of nuclear deterrence policy, made in light of John Paul II's evaluation, but applying it through our own prudential judgments, lead us to a strictly conditioned moral acceptance of nuclear deterrence. We cannot consider it adequate as a long-term basis for peace" (p. 58).

Devoid of modifiers, the judgment on deterrence is "acceptance," not "condemnation." But the acceptance is "strictly conditioned." This phrase places two kinds of restraint on the strategy of deterrence. The first is "temporal" in nature; both John Paul II, in his address to the United Nations in 1982, and the American bishops tie the justification for deterrence to an understanding that it be used as a framework for moving to a different basis of security among nations. This temporal assessment means that the "direction" of deterrence policy has moral significance: are steps being taken to move away from this fragile, paradoxical basis for interstate relations, or is the direction of policy simply reinforcing the present state of affairs?

The second restraint concerns the "character" of the deterrent. The strictly conditioned justification of the deterrent rests upon its role of preventing the use of nuclear weapons or other actions that could lead directly to a nuclear exchange. The point here is to limit the role of nuclear deterrence to a specific function in world affairs; the posture of deterrence is not to be used to pursue other goals than preventing nuclear war. To give specific content to this limited conception of deterrence, the bishops make a series of concrete proposals.

They oppose: (1) extending deterrence to a variety of warfighting strategies; (2) a quest for strategic superiority; (3) any blurring of the distinction between nuclear and conventional weapons; and (4) the deployment of weapons with hard-target kill capability.

They support: (1) immediate, bilateral, verifiable agreements to halt the testing, production, and deployment of new nuclear systems; (2) negotiating strategies aimed at deep cuts in superpower arsenals; (3) conclusion of a comprehensive test ban treaty; and (4) strengthening of command and control systems for nuclear weapons.

Although an extensive commentary, both empirical and ethical, has been generated about the specific positions *The Challenge of Peace* espoused, the primary significance of the pastoral letter has been to provide space in the public argument for moral analysis. This analysis, however, is not unanimous; there are positions to the left and right of the pastoral letter. The complexity of the nuclear question and public debate surrounding it is intensified when the appeal is made to ethical as well as empirical data. At least three other moral arguments can be contrasted with *The Challenge of Peace.* One is a strategic-moral case; the second a political-moral position; the third a technological-moral argument.

The strategic-moral argument has two versions, one to the right of the pastoral and one to the left of it, but they share a similar style. Professor Albert Wohlstetter, an original and prolific contributor to the empirical literature on strategy, wrote an extensive commentary on the pastoral letter, which affirmed its basic moral principles but disagreed vigorously with its policy conclusions.

> By revising many times in public their pastoral letter on war and peace, American Catholic bishops have dramatized the moral issue which statesmen, using empty threats to end the world, neglect or evade. For the bishops stand in a long moral tradition which condemns the threat to destroy innocents as well as their actual destruction. They try but do not escape reliance on threatening bystanders. . . . But because the bishops must take threats seriously, they make more visible the essential evasions of Western statesmen. (Wohlstetter, 1983, p. 15)

Wohlstetter was entirely in support of the pastoral's emphasis on the principle of noncombatant immunity, but he
felt the bishops had squandered a unique moral opportunity
by failing to follow the logic of the moral principle through
to proper policy conclusions. The misstep in the letter is its
reliance on secular technical judgments, which contend that
the use of nuclear weapons cannot be controlled. In Wohlstetter's view, such empirical judgments are technologically
dated, lead to misguided strategic conclusions, and erode the
moral case that can be made for a justifiable nuclear doctrine: "The bishops, their defenders and the strategists on
whom they rely all talk of the uncontrollability of nuclear
weapons as a deplorable but unavoidable fact of life. . . .
However, it would be naive or worse to suppose that we cannot impose controls over both initial and subsequent uses of
nuclear weapons" (Wohlstetter, 1983, pp. 15, 26).

Wohlstetter's confidence in our recent and growing ability
to meet the moral criteria of limits on force is based on both
the increasing accuracy of nuclear (and conventional) weapons and the miniaturization of warheads, which reduces both
blast effect and fallout. These technological developments can
and should lead to a strategic and targeting doctrine focused
not on civilian populations but on those targets that the Soviets really value: centers of their political and military power.
Such a targeting doctrine would be a far more effective deterrent than explicit or implied threats to strike the civilian
population of the Soviet Union. The moral virtue of this
technological-strategic shift is that it shifts deterrence policy
away from a twenty-year trend of fixation on civilian targets
and places it within the justifiable limits of classical moral
teaching. In sum, a clear recognition of what is technologically feasible today should have led the bishops, and should
lead others, to a deterrence policy that is both strategically
more effective and morally legitimate. The bishops forfeited
a chance to move the strategic debate in this direction because of a lack of consistency between the moral principles
they taught and the policy recommendations they espoused.

A very different strategic-moral critique of the nuclear

question that also finds the pastoral letter inconsistent comes from Professor Susan M. Okins (1984). In her view the moral principles of the pastoral should have led to a strict nuclear pacifism. In direct contrast to Wohlstetter's position favoring a more usable deterrent, Okin argues that no deterrent can meet the classical moral criteria and that the only viable moral course is withdrawal from a strategy of deterrence.

> All in all, if we take seriously the evidence they cite, the questions the bishops raise about the real possibility of limiting a nuclear exchange all require clear negative answers. . . . Nuclear disarmament is the only logical conclusion of the bishops' arguments, and it is avoided by them only by means of ambiguity and inconsistency.
> (Okin, 1984, pp. 536, 553)

Okin's convictions about the uncontrollability of nuclear weapons so dominate her argument that she judges the sliver of ambiguity on use found in the pastoral letter a fundamental moral flaw, and she terms any efforts to redirect nuclear weapons away from civilians toward military targets a perversion of moral reasoning. For Okin there is no technological or strategic route to rectify the moral bankruptcy of deterrence.

The Wohlstetter-Okin responses to the pastoral letter exemplify a pervasive strand in the nuclear debate about the intersection of ethical and empirical data. Wohlstetter's confidence about precise, technological control of nuclear weapons and his willingness to increase the capacity of both superpowers to strike each other's military targets dispose too quickly of the contention that a very delicate line of fact and perception exists between a credible counterforce deterrent and a posture that can increase the likelihood of nuclear war. The latter can occur either because of the confidence one party has in controlled use or because one's adversary mistakes a threat of controlled use for a first-strike strategy and is then tempted to make a preemptive attack. Okin's conclusion that delegitimation of the deterrent is the only morally acceptable strategy too quickly dispenses with the possibility that drastic moves to delegitimate the deterrence posture of one party will lead to a string of misperceptions and miscalculations, ending in the use of nuclear weapons.

Both criticisms of the consistency of the pastoral letter share the conviction that a direct, unambiguous, and inflexible link must exist between the moral evaluation of use and that of deterrence policy. The essence of the strategic-moral problem is that *some* link must be maintained between use and deterrence doctrine. *The Challenge of Peace* seeks to draw a line between the two dimensions of nuclear policy, but the bishops do not share either the technological confidence of Wohlstetter on use or the absolutism of Okin on deterrence.

The strategic-moral argument focuses on "just means" of nuclear policy; the political-moral argument focuses on the relationship of ends and means. Once again two responses to the pastoral—this time, complementary views—highlight the meaning of the political-moral argument. Both Michael Novak and the French Catholic bishops frame the nuclear ethics question in a different way than *The Challenge of Peace;* they define the primary moral problem of the nuclear age as the clash of political ideologies and objectives embodied in U.S.-Soviet competition. Although acknowledging that nuclear weapons are not simply like others, they cast the nuclear question primarily in terms of "just cause" issues. Novak writes, "Virtually all arguments about the prevention of nuclear war hinge on judgments concerning the nature of the Soviet Union and its nuclear forces" (Novak, 1983, p. 49). This means for him that "religious leaders who wish to influence public policy by influencing public opinion owe a special debt to democratic states and incur an obligation to defend them against those who would destroy them" (p. 48). The disparity in "just cause" between East and West should be the explicit context within which the means of policy are examined. The position of both Novak and the French bishops blunts the critique of deterrence. The essence of the French letter is captured in the phrase "Between War and Blackmail." The phrase is meant to say that both ends and means must be evaluated, but the thrust of the French letter is on the dangers of not taking the political threat seriously. Thus the French ask: "Would not an unconditional refusal to defend oneself provide an opportunity for blackmail? A nuclear war would annihilate the earth, but is it necessary, for the sake of saving the peace, to give up our liberty, our dignity?" (Schall, 1984).

The U.S. bishops recognize the ends-means problem of the nuclear age, but they weigh the factors of the moral equation differently. The political competition of the superpowers is both a decisive fact of world politics today and a reflection of a historical constant in international relations. From the Peloponnesian Wars through the European balance of power to U.S.-Soviet relations, states have competed for territory, possessions, and influence. The distinctive feature of the nuclear age—what sets it apart from the narrative of politics and war stretching from the Greeks to World War II— is the means by which the traditional political contest is now adjudicated.

The perspective of *The Challenge of Peace* is that nuclear weapons pose a direct, definitive threat to the very political values that have justified resort to force in the past. Although the U.S. pastoral does not adopt the Okin prescription of nuclear pacifism, it finds deterrence justified only for the purpose of preventing nuclear war. Other dimensions of the U.S.-Soviet rivalry are to be managed in nonnuclear terms. While neither Novak nor the French bishops advocate the use of nuclear weapons, the effect of the U.S. bishops' letter is to be more stringent in its critique of nuclear deterrence and nuclear diplomacy.

The technological-moral argument about nuclear policy finds its clearest expression in the supporters of SDI. President Reagan makes his case for SDI with a strong moral component, which is also reflected in the arguments of other advocates of defensive systems. The moral argument for SDI is usually made in terms of its *purpose* (to target weapons, not people) and its *goal* (to transcend deterrence—at least this is the declared final goal). Phrased in this way, the *intentions* of the SDI advocates appear beyond criticism. But the SDI debate raises precisely the moral question of balancing *intentions and consequences* in the moral judgment of a policy. In principle most participants in the nuclear debate want to go "beyond deterrence." The key question is how to pursue this goal. Although it is difficult to disagree with the intentions of the sDI supporters, it is not difficult to raise serious, substantial questions about the consequences and risks of pursuing the sDI course. There are enormous technological problems in making the system work, and there is the fundamental issue of the transition from an offensive to a defensive system. Without detailing the specifics of the transition problem, it can be summarized in the fear that rather than transcending or enhancing deterrence, the pursuit of defensive systems will fuel an offensive-defensive race at enormous cost and great danger to the stability of the already risky deterrence balance. The process of balancing intentions versus consequences is one of the points in the nuclear debate where the intersection of ethical and empirical data becomes crucially important. Precisely because good intentions are not sufficient to make good policy, the assessment of risks and possible consequences in scientific, strategic, and technological terms becomes a crucial ingredient in the moral equation.

From this constricted assessment of several forms of the moral argument made in the nuclear debate, it is clear that while most people agree the nuclear issue is a moral problem, there are substantial differences in how the problem is to be defined and decided. The moral questions raise issues that are not addressed if the debate stays only in the framework of hard data. But the moral questions also require a return to empirical arguments if the moral response is to be made about policy judgments. The nuclear winter enters the public debate as a product of scientific investigation. But its impact is to intensify several of the moral problems already embedded in the nuclear argument. The nuclear winter proposition expands the scope of potential victims, heightens the perception of risk in the nuclear stalemate, erodes the conviction that nuclear weapons can be understood as rational instruments of policy, and reinforces the judgment of *The Challenge of Peace* that deterrence is not a long-term solution to the nuclear problem. Not all participants will draw the same moral conclusions from the nuclear winter, but no moral argument will be unaffected by it. What follows is one analyst's method of relating the ethical and empirical data.

The Policy Implications of the Ethical and Empirical Data

The convergence of ethical and empirical analyses of the nuclear threat points to some policy guidelines. The first lesson both the evidence of science and the wisdom of ethics teach is the danger of conventional thinking when faced with a revolutionary danger. The findings of the nuclear winter research help us to appreciate the utterly unprecedented situation the nuclear age has created. For over twenty years the public and policymakers have lived with the knowledge that a nuclear exchange between the superpowers would be suicidal. Now we find that the use of nuclear weapons by only one side could be catastrophic in its consequences for the user and the rest of humanity. Our choices are even more constrained than we once believed. The fact that we have lived through four decades of the nuclear age in ignorance of just how precarious the human situation is should make us even more aware of what we do not yet know about the danger in which we live.

To warn against conventional thinking is to do more than make a self-evident statement. Nothing is more rooted in the conventional wisdom of the nuclear policy debate than the double conviction that deterrence "has worked" for forty years and therefore it is the best we can do. These assumptions often produce the attitude that those who call attention to the fragility, uncertainty, or folly of aspects of deterrence policy are the real threats to our public welfare. To yield to this attitude would be fundamentally wrong. I realize that it is easier to criticize deterrence than to construct an alternative. But the nuclear winter discussion highlights in devastatingly dramatic terms why none of us should be content with the status quo.

A second lesson to be drawn from the ethical and empirical data is the need to move the public and policy discussion beyond a general awareness of the danger of the nuclear age to a consensus on some key policy imperatives. The response to the nuclear winter evidence highlights a public that has become much more sensitive to the realities of the nuclear age. But awareness will not move us beyond our present condition unless we can build a broad-based coalition which may not agree on the details of a new policy but could agree on some fundamental guidelines. Currently we do not have such agreement in the body politic. Although the Yankelovitch article documents significant shifts in public perception of the nuclear danger, it also illustrates severe splits between the public and policy elites on what should be done. One objective of the bishops' pastoral letter was to bridge the discussion in the policy and popular debates. Without some core consensus on policy prescriptions, discussion of the danger of the nuclear age may lead to paralysis rather than a creative response.

I will outline four prescriptions for a public consensus. For them to be effectively translated into policy, support would have to be visible in both the popular and the policy communities. My sense is that it will be more difficult to sell this package in the policy community, even though there is hardly anything here that is drastically new.

First, the primary objective of our nuclear policy should be to ensure that these weapons are not used, by us or by others. The proposition reflects all the paradoxes of nuclear strategy. It reflects on the one hand the truth first stated by Bernard Brodie, one of the nation's foremost nuclear strategists, when he said in 1946 that nuclear weapons were unusable in any rational policy. It is a truth reaffirmed by former Secretary of Defense Robert S. McNamara as recently as 1983. But the policy proposition reflects on the other hand the reality that nuclear weapons will be with us for the foreseeable future. To set a policy objective of nonuse means to presuppose that use is always a possibility. Hence a policy of nonuse is not simply a product of not wanting to use nuclear weapons. To take seriously the policy prescription of nonuse as a *goal* of policy, it will be necessary to shape our strategic doctrine, our deployment policies, even our targeting doctrine in light of the prior premise of nonuse. Weapons like the MX or the Soviet SS-18s and SS-19s, which intensify the temptation to use in a crisis, run counter to the policy prescription of nonuse. So do strategic doctrines of launch-on-warning or launch-under-attack; so do plans to target either side's command and control facilities. To accept nonuse as a goal of policy requires public support for a series of policy choices that will reinforce a nonuse posture.

Second, arms control policy should be designed to cap the arms race immediately and then to follow with deep cuts in both superpower arsenals. Once again, although no one will come forward in the popular or policy debate in favor of escalation of the arms race, getting a consensus on the objective of capping the competition is very difficult. The arguments made against it include the criticism that it will freeze the United States in an inferior position to the Soviets, that it will foster instability in the deterrence relationship, and that it will prevent needed modernization of the deterrence forces. There is a case to be made on each of these points, but there is also another case to be made that arms control for most of the nuclear age has been vulnerable to the proposal that we need "one more system" for either safety or security before we cap the arms race. A policy that moved from capping the race immediately to cuts on both sides aimed not only at reducing the number of weapons but at achieving some parity in the arsenals could, I believe, address the concerns raised in the criticisms against capping the race now. A goal of putting an absolute cap on the vertical proliferation of the superpower competition could have a dramatic political and psychological effect on the superpowers and on others in the international community not unlike the impact of Anwar Sadat's visit to Jerusalem. It could provide a breakthrough that creates political space for steps to reverse the escalation and begin the search for stable deterrence at much lower levels of arms. To reverse the dynamic of the arms race is the first step toward ridding the world of the threat posed by nuclear winter.

Third, to enhance the possibilities of a sustained effort to reverse the arms race, both superpowers should insulate nuclear arms control from the other dimensions of their political competition. This policy prescription is based on a dual assertion: first, that the superpower relationship will continue to be conflicted in a variety of areas, and, second, that the nuclear competition is qualitatively different in its danger for the superpowers and for the world from other dimensions of the superpower relationship. Essentially this policy prescription calls for a very loose doctrine of "linkage." That is to say, we should not mortgage the possibilities of progress on nuclear arms because of differences with the Soviet Union on Central America, Afghanistan, or the Horn of Africa. Each of these other questions is very important and needs to be addressed on its own terms. There are lives being lost, human rights being violated, and economies being ravaged in each case, but the very high chance that the two superpowers will disagree strongly on these and a host of other issues in the foreseeable future means that nuclear arms control should not be hostage to these other conflicts. Very often it is the public that stresses the linkage phenomenon when it becomes aware of Soviet activity on some issue. We need an explicit public and policy debate aimed at trying to fashion a consensus against a strong doctrine of linkage.

Fourth, precisely because bilaterally negotiated restraints on the arms race are so difficult to obtain and take so long to ratify, there should be a policy prescription that encourages prudent, carefully calculated "independent initiatives" which could be tried periodically. Such initiatives are steps that could be taken by the United States (or the Soviet Union) without mortally threatening the deterrence capacity of the initiating side. The step would be announced and a time limit attached to it. If the other side did not respond in some reciprocal fashion within the time limit, then the initiative could be withdrawn. Such a process of independent initiatives provides a complement to the normal method of bilateral negotiations.

At first glance, in the face of the dangers outlined in the nuclear winter scenario, all four of these steps seem simple—

well worth the risk to avoid nuclear use and to reverse the
arms race. But currently none of them is clearly supported
in either the popular or the policy debate. A consensus around
these measures will have to be created—it does not exist at
present.

The creation of a public consensus with the political
strength and strategic specificity to move the nuclear relationship in a new direction will require a mix of many voices
and the support of diverse constituencies. The nuclear debate of the 1980s has already joined some allies with quite
different starting points and some past differences. The nuclear winter argument creates a fascinating convergence of
scientific and religious insight. The U.S. bishops addressed
their congregations as "the first generation since Genesis" with
the ability to threaten the created order. The scientific community is now spelling out the details of this threat. The expected (in many quarters) tension or opposition between religion and science is transformed by the stakes of the nuclear
equation into an alliance that struggles to prevent the destruction of the world and its most precious element, the human family.

References

Bundy, M., Kennan, G. F., McNamara, R. S., & Smith, G. (1982).
Nuclear weapons and the Atlantic alliance. *Foreign Affairs, 60,*
753–768.

Gremillion, J. (1976). *The gospel of peace and justice: Catholic teaching
since Pope John.* Maryknoll, NY: Orbis Press.

Kaiser, K., Leber, G., Mertes, A., & Schulze, F. J. (1982). Nuclear
weapons and the preservation of peace. *Foreign Affairs, 60,*
1157–1170.

The National Conference of Catholic Bishops. (1983). *The challenge of peace: God's promise and our response.* Washington, DC:
U.S. Catholic Conference.

Novak, M. (1983). *Moral clarity in the nuclear age.* Nashville, TN:
Thomas Nelson Publishers.

Okin, S. (1984). Taking the bishops seriously. *World Politics, 36,*
527–554.

Schall, J. (Ed.). (1984). *Winning the peace: Joint pastoral letter of the French bishops.* San Francisco: Ignatius Press.

Wohlstetter, A. (1983, June). Bishops, statesmen and other strategists on the bombing of innocents. *Commentary.*

Yankelovitch, D., & Doble, J. (1984). The public mood. *Foreign Affairs, 60,* 1157–1170.

Afterword: Nuclear Winter and the Will to Power

JEROME D. FRANK

The nuclear arsenals of the superpowers have for many years contained enough destructive capacity to wipe out Western civilization. The discovery of the two nations' ability to jeopardize all life on earth, so convincingly described by Carl Sagan, has intensified the urgency of finding ways to prevent a nuclear holocaust. Responding to the initiative of Lester Grinspoon, the contributions to this book have explored aspects of the virtually limitless destructive power of nuclear weapons from the standpoints of history, psychiatry, developmental psychology, biology, and theology. In this final chapter, I propose to consider a feature of human nature that may be the greatest threat to our survival: the will to power. In addition, I shall consider some of the topics brought up by the other contributors and some further implications for preventing a nuclear disaster.

Power is implicit in all human relationships. The universality of power struggles between groups is inherent in Erikson's concept of pseudospeciation, supplemented by Gould's biological perspective.

A major aspect of the pursuit of power has always been the effort to achieve destructive capacity greater than that of potential or actual adversaries. This effort has finally been crowned by the invention of nuclear weaponry, the ultimate expression of destructiveness. Lifton provides an illuminating and stimulating commentary on some general psychological implications of the horrendous destructive power of nuclear weapons, based on reports of those few humans who have actually experienced their effects. Mack examines some of the psychological ramifications of power in a nuclear world, exemplified by his discussions of "the shibboleth of national security" and "ideologies of enmity."

The relations between power and morality are considered by Commager and Hehir. Commager, from the perspective

of an historian, shows how morality has been pressed into the
service of power through the venerable doctrine of Reason
of State. And, finally, Hehir, a theologian, explores the moral
as well as practical unacceptability of nuclear weapons as instruments of national power.

The Will to Power

Why do leaders of the nuclear superpowers, who are typ-
ically intelligent, well-balanced, reasonable people, urge the
accumulation of nuclear weapons far in excess of any conceivable military usefulness, with increasing danger to the
entire planet, despite the warnings of retired military offi-
cers, including commanders in chief, and highly placed civilian leaders?

An explanation for this potentially suicidal behavior, one
favored by many psychologists and political leaders, is that it
is motivated primarily by fear of the opponent (R. K. White,
1984). According to this view, the United States and the Soviet Union both pursue the illusory goal of nuclear weapons
superiority primarily to deter the other from using them.
Mutual deterrence, however, has long since been achieved in
that only a small fraction of current nuclear arsenals on the
invulnerable submarines of one nation can destroy the other.
Accumulating additional nuclear weapons adds nothing to
security but contributes to a new source of anxiety created
by the weapons themselves; for the greater the number of
these weapons, the greater the danger of their inadvertent
discharge, with potentially catastrophic consequences.

A more sophisticated version of deterrence is that to be
effective it must include the ability to respond in a flexible,
controlled manner if the other side initiates nuclear hostili-
ties at any level or in any form; thus for effective deterrence
each side must possess a wide range of nuclear weapons and
delivery systems. This so-called war-fighting doctrine, which
rests on the assumption that a nuclear war could be limited,
flies in the face of judgments by highest level military and
civilian experts that limited nuclear war is "a chimera" (Lee,
1982).

Accordingly, if the sole purpose of the nuclear arms race were to allay mutual anxieties, it should have ended after each side possessed a minimum invulnerable deterrent. Each nation would be more secure with a handful of invulnerable nuclear submarines able to destroy the other than with the present wide proliferation of nuclear weapons.

We must look beyond mutual fears, then, to find the causes of the runaway nuclear arms race. Many of these causes, including features of bureaucracies and the vast number of jobs and huge economic investments dependent on pursuit of the nuclear arms race, although clearly important, lie beyond the scope of my presentation. Of the psychological forces involved, perhaps the most important is the will to power. In fact, a major source of the anxiety that stimulates arms races is the fear by each side that the other's drive for power may lead it to launch an attack.

The will to power stimulates violence because of its relationship to the emotions of fear and anger. For both individuals and groups, anger caused by frustration gives rise to the urge to destroy its source. Fear stimulates violence in the individual against the source of threat if the frightened individual feels cornered. A group becomes violent in response to a threat to its continued identity as a group.

A power-seeking group will inevitably eventually come up against another group dominated by the same motive, leading to a confrontation in which each threatens and frustrates the other. The resulting mutual fear and rage may lead to violence.

One must add that the role of emotions in influencing decisions of national leaders is hard to evaluate. Emotions have been shown to influence leaders' behavior in crises where rapid decisions had to be made under conditions of extreme tension (George, 1985). By and large, however, leaders are among the most emotionally stable members of their societies because in order to reach the top they must have weathered many emotionally stressful situations. Moreover, decisions of heads of state to go to war are ostensibly based on highly rational calculations (Howard, 1984). On the other hand, emotions can influence apparently rational decisions of national leaders in subtle ways (Janis, in press). Emotional reactions almost certainly contribute to the frequent misinterpretations by leaders of antagonistic groups of each other's capabilities and intentions.

The power drive as such has not played much part in psychiatric thinking except for Adler (Ansbacher & Ansbacher, 1956) and Horney (1950). One can speculate as to the possible reasons for this neglect. Certainly the power drive is not lacking in psychologists and psychiatrists themselves, as anyone who has attended meetings of professional societies or academic committees knows. The striving for power per se, however, is usually not consistent with the major sources of self-esteem in academicians and clinicians. For the former, power is expressed in the ability to design experiments, express ideas, and the like; for the latter, in helping suffering people. Furthermore, no patient comes to a clinician seeking help for an excessive will to power, although the clinicians may indeed decide that that is the source of some patients' distress.

Insofar as the power drive enters into the thinking of psychiatrists, it is in relation to psychopathology, as in such concepts as infantile omnipotence or narcissism. Erich Fromm's definition of narcissism will serve as well as any other: "a state of experience in which only the person himself . . . [is] experienced as fully real while everybody and everything that does not form part of the person or is not an object of his needs . . . [is] affectively without weight and color" (Fromm, 1973, p. 201).

The relative neglect of the will to power as a component of normal personality by psychologists and psychiatrists is the more surprising in that it has long been a preoccupation of historians, anthropologists, philosophers, and theologians. Tacitus called the lust for power "the most flagrant of all the passions" (Tuchman, 1984, p. 381). Commager, as already noted, examines the power drive of nations as manifested in the doctrine of Reason of State and notes the centrality of this concept in the philosophy of Hegel, among others. The anthropologist Andrew Schmookler has pointed out that if for any reason one group decides to try to impose its will on another, the latter has no choice except to respond within the framework of power. "No one is free to choose peace, but anyone can impose on all the necessity for power" (Schmookler, 1984, p. 21).

For the theologian Reinhold Niebuhr, the drive for power is one manifestation of pride, "the basic sin." As he puts it: "Man . . . seeks to overcome his insecurity by a will-to-power which overreaches the limits of human creatureliness. . . . Man is tempted, in other words, to break and transcend the limits which God has set for him" (Niebuhr, 1949, pp. 178, 180). This thought is echoed by Bertrand Russell: "While animals are content with existence and reproduction, men desire also to expand, and their desires in this respect are limited only by what imagination suggests as possible. Every man would like to be God" (Russell, 1948, p. 10).

Niebuhr's view of pride as the basic sin, translated into secular terms, can be taken to mean that the very trait that has enabled humans to dominate the rest of creation contains the seeds of our self-destruction. Humans have always viewed as praiseworthy efforts to extend their power over the inanimate world, the animate world, and their fellow humans. With respect to the first two, we have succeeded in achieving virtually godlike powers to create and destroy. In attempting to dominate one another, however, we are now threatening to bring on mutual annihilation.

According to Niebuhr, the pride of power is supported by moral pride and the pride of intellect. Moral pride, or self-righteousness, is "the pretension of finite man that . . . his very relative moral standards are absolute" (Niebuhr, 1949, p. 199). His concept of moral pride reminds us of Commager's description of how societies always claim moral justification for actions based on Reason of State. The pride of intellect leads to the conviction that the human intellect can solve any problem. In the context of the nuclear arms race, intellectual pride is manifested in the unwarranted belief of nuclear experts that their scenarios for limited, controlled use of nuclear weapons in battle would actually work.

The drive for power is fundamental to life in the sense that all living creatures must control aspects of their environment in order to survive. In humans this drive may have deep psychological roots in that infants control the behavior of their mothers. If mothers were not programmed to respond to the infant's signals of distress, and in this sense to submit to the infant's control, the infant would soon perish.

In any case, at a very early age children seek deliberately to control persons and objects in the environment, an activity attributed by the psychologist Robert W. White to what he calls "effectance motivation" (R. W. White, 1959), which he rightly ranks as a primary drive. Like all behavior in the service of effectance motivation, the exercise of power is inherently highly pleasurable. The glee a child experiences from getting a toy to work, an actor's exhiliration after a successful performance, a leader's exultation at crushing a rival—all may be expressions of the same drive toward mastery.

In the form of ambition, the will to power is probably the major psychological source of all human achievement. Without ambition, humans would lack motivation continually to strive to better themselves and to persist in overcoming obstacles toward achievement of their goals. The irony is that the very drive that has enabled humans to dominate the nonliving and animal worlds and to reach high levels of civilization threatens to destroy us when it is aimed at fellow humans, and when it becomes exacerbated by a sense of insecurity, to which it is an effective antidote.

The Will to Power in Leaders

With the development of the power to think conceptually, individuals inevitably become aware of their fundamental vulnerability and fragility, including their mortality. Thanks to their symbolic powers, humans are able to deal with this chilling recognition in many ways that are rarely fully conscious or clearly articulated. Existential anxiety can be overcome by religious faith, artistic creativity, and scholarly productivity, among other things. It may be that those who choose to seek leadership, whatever their other motives, are trying to overcome feelings of insecurity and helplessness arising from the existential predicament by aggrandizing themselves and the groups with which they identify. As Niebuhr suggests, power becomes the means by which leaders seek to overcome their "creatureliness"—that is, their sense of mortality. Images of their place in history motivate the behavior of many leaders, especially as they age. For those who rely on the acquisition of power or its equivalent, wealth, as the chief antidote to existential fear, the will to power is insatiable—the wealthy person never has enough money, and the leader never has enough power. Possession of all the money and power in the world would not overcome the possessor's existential insignificance.

Crucial to the peace of mind of all leaders is the belief that they can control events under their jurisdictions, whether these events are caused primarily by people or by impersonal forces such as economic conditions and technological innovations. Furthermore, most leaders are optimistic by temperament—that is, they believe they can prevail. The more successful a leader is, the more his belief has been reinforced—that is, leaders who reach the top have by definition experienced more victories than defeats. The greater the number of a leader's past successes, the stronger his expectation of future ones. If the leader is a political figure, his belief in his ability to control events is reinforced by the adulation of his followers.

The effort to overcome existential insecurity, pleasure in domination, and optimism based on past successes may contribute to the fact that so many great leaders (Napoleon and Hitler come to mind) continue to seek to subjugate lands and peoples until they overreach themselves.

The attributes of a successful leader are control of the means of power and a strong will to prevail. In the anarchic international arena, the chief means of power is weaponry, so contestants seek to intimidate their rivals by demonstrating that they have both superior weaponry and greater resoluteness, steadfastness, or strength of will.

Strength of resolve may sometimes be more important a determinant of the outcome of conflicts than the possession of superior weaponry. Hitler invaded the Rhineland, for example, in the face of vastly stronger French military forces, whose leaders, however, lacked the will to resist him. A more recent example is the victory of the North Vietnamese in the face of enormously greater U.S. military power, largely because the United States gradually lost the will to accept the hardships, dislocations, and deaths involved in continuing the war.

The importance of the role of will in international struggles is demonstrated by the fact that conflicts often continue long after their initial cause has vanished. Prolongation of senseless conflict occurs when the determination to prove that one's will is stronger than that of the adversary becomes more important than gaining the goal over which the struggle rages. A tragic example was the terrible and relentless struggle for Verdun in World War I, which, according to a military historian, continued after its "strategic significance . . . had long since passed out of sight; yet the battle had somehow achieved a demonic existence of its own far beyond the control of generals of either nation" (Horne, 1966, p. 42).

As in this example, the ultimate test of stronger will is being prepared to undergo hardship and suffering, even to risk one's own survival, in order to defeat one's rival, a factor that is clearly involved in the nuclear arms race.

Although, before the advent of nuclear weapons, efforts by nations to acquire larger and more technologically advanced arsenals than those of their adversaries were objectively justifiable, the investment of vast resources in this endeavor was also a means of demonstrating national resolve. In this connection, the American reliance on achievement of technological superiority over the Soviet Union in the nuclear arms race is reinforced by a general faith in technological solutions, as described by Mack. In view of the American record of technological achievement, faith in a technological solution to the nuclear arms race at first glance may seem justified, but in reality it is an illusion based on intellectual pride. To be sure, one cannot be certain that even so complicated a scheme as the Star Wars project is unachievable. The search for technological fixes is justified to the extent that humans have solved many problems that experts at the time "knew" to be insoluble—a striking example being the splitting of the atom. Problems posed by nature, however, differ in a fundamental way from those created by fellow humans—nature does not fight back. Although armaments may present technical challenges, they are basically human ones. The ability to innovate technologically is not the exclusive property of only one of the rivals. Each simultaneously tries to develop weapons that would penetrate the other's defenses and to create defenses that are impenetrable to the other's weapons. The same mental processes are utilized to pursue both goals. Although one side or the other may gain a temporary lead, inevitably the other catches up. It is true that adequate defenses have been developed in time against all conventional weapons, but none has ever been perfect, and the defenses were adequate only because the destructive power of these weapons was limited. Since the destructive capacity of nuclear weapons is unlimited, to be effective against them a defense would have to be virtually perfect, and this goal has never been achieved and, it is safe to say, never will be.

In all arms races leaders of both sides seek not only to acquire more destructive weapons than their adversaries but to develop new and more effective ones. Since their inventors can never be sure whether the new weapons will really work until they are tried in battle, this creates what has been called the technological imperative: if a weapon is invented, it must be built, and if it is built, it must be used.

The Will to Power and Nuclear Weapons

With conventional weapons, seeking to acquire larger and more sophisticated weapons as the way to intimidate a potential enemy without war if possible, and to win a war if one occurred, made sense for two reasons. One is that all the effort and ingenuity in the world could not create arsenals big enough to endanger the continuance of civilization, much less produce a catastrophe of the magnitude of a nuclear winter. The other is that, as Mack has pointed out, conventional weapons increased a nation's strength and security in reality as well as in appearance: the more a nation possessed, the stronger and more secure it really was, and there was no limit to this process.

Nuclear weapons, because of their limitless destructive power, have fundamentally changed this state of affairs. They have permanently broken the connection between weaponry and strength in one respect, but not in another. Perception and reality still coincide in that the strategic nuclear weapons of one adversary gravely menace the other. Reality differs sharply from perception, however, in that, beyond a level long since passed by the United States and the Soviet Union, accumulating more powerful and sophisticated strategic nuclear weapons decreases the security of all nations, including the possessors. Nuclear weapons beyond the point of mutual overkill convey strength in appearance only. In fact, the larger the number of nuclear weapons in a nation's arsenal, the greater the fear it inspires in actual or potential enemies, thereby heightening the danger of a weapon's being fired through miscalculation or mischance. Increasing the number and sophistication of nuclear weapons thus paradoxically increases the insecurity of their possessors.

Since nuclear weapons cannot actually be used against another nuclear power without enormous risk of destruction to the user, their remaining function is to demonstrate superior will. So the nuclear powers seek to intimidate each other by building ever more costly and elaborate nuclear weapons, regardless of their military usefulness. The argument that failure to deploy the MX missile, for example, would be seen by the Russians as a sign of weakness of will persuaded Congress for a while to finance the continued building of these missiles despite any pretense of military justification for them.

Moreover, to demonstrate resolve, it is necessary not only to maintain a large nuclear arsenal but to continually improve it. This line of reasoning supplies the motive for an endless arms race in which in essence the different branches of the military within each country compete with one another, regardless of what the adversary does.

Conceptual Inertia

The major psychological reason for continuing behavior that has clearly become maladaptive may be termed force of habit, or "conceptual inertia" (Rapoport, 1984). When humans are faced with an entirely new and unprecedented problem such as the abrupt emergence of nuclear weapons, they try to make it appear like a familiar problem and to handle it by methods that worked with the latter. National leaders have reached their positions of prominence by virtue of their success in handling international relations in a world of conventional weapons. In that world it was appropriate for the leaders of every nation to seek to acquire more and better weapons than its actual or potential adversaries in order to deter them from acting against the nation's interests or, should deterrence fail, to win the resulting war. Since all wars since World War II have been fought exclusively with conventional weapons, this habitual pattern has continued to be reinforced, even though national leaders know intellectually that in a nuclear world "comprehensive military supremacy for either side is a military and economic impossibility" (Brown, 1980, p. 3).

Furthermore, since time immemorial military leaders have made detailed plans for campaigns and battles that sought to anticipate and take care of all possible contingencies. Even though in the carnage and confusion of battle these plans were seldom carried out exactly as drawn up, to the extent that errors did not result in total disaster the plans were useful guides. Obeying the force of habit, military planners of nuclear nations today continue to draw up elaborate scenarios for limited, controlled nuclear war. To be successful, such plans would require perfect minute-by-minute command and control of complex electronic systems untested in battle. At the same time, in mid-exchange, with decisive time intervals measured in minutes and seconds, leaders of both adversaries, while under unimaginable emotional tensions, would have to communicate constantly in order to work out agreed ways of stopping short of total destruction. Merely stating these requirements makes it obvious that the chances for successfully implementing scenarios for limited nuclear war are infinitesimal; yet such is the pride of intellect that weapons experts continue to prepare them. Just as nuclear weapons create only the illusion of strength, nuclear scenarios create only the illusion of control.

In this connection, as Mack has pointed out, the prospect of a nuclear winter, far from causing leaders to abandon nuclear weapons, has stimulated them to attempt to refine the weapons and retarget them in such a way as to be able to destroy the opponent's military capabilities while their total explosive power remains under the threshold of nuclear winter—an effort that is manifestly absurd.

The Trap of Words

The conceptual inertia that causes leaders to continue to think about nuclear weapons as if they were conventional ones is reinforced by language (Frank, 1982). Reality is to an extraordinary extent what we tell ourselves it is (Rapoport, 1984). Until the advent of television, we experienced only those aspects of reality that impinged directly on our sense organs. The multitude of events out of range of our senses were experienced only through what we read or what others told us. Television has expanded the range of sight and hearing, but the information we receive in this way, in addition to being highly selective and filtered through the words of the commentators, still accounts for only a tiny part of the information that shapes our ways of thinking. Words, furthermore, are the only transmitters of features of culture that have no sensory component. These features include moral values, worldviews, and the like.

Since we think by means of words and the associations they conjure up, the use of inappropriate words to think about a problem condemns us to reach wrong conclusions almost before we know we have started to think.

Our perception of the nature of nuclear weapons has been largely shaped by words. These weapons have burst upon the world so recently that we have not had time to develop an appropriate vocabulary for them. Hence we have fallen back on words that were appropriate to the world of prenuclear weapons, but that now lead us seriously astray. We speak automatically of "nuclear war"—yet a nuclear holocaust would differ from all previous wars in crucial ways. For Americans at least, war conjures up the image of struggles, highly destructive, to be sure, but conducted far from home by specially trained cadres. Furthermore, wars have made the United States the richest and most powerful nation on earth. Although European nations have known the ravages of war firsthand—and these have been terrible—these ravages would not be in the same league as the destruction created by a nuclear exchange. Up to now, damage to the ecology by war has ceased after the last weapon was fired, enabling the environment to restore itself. But long after the last nuclear weapon had been discharged, release of radioactive substances, depletion of the ozone layer, destruction of forests, and erosion of soil would continue to wreak ecological havoc.

By using the word *war* to describe such a catastrophe, we also conjure up the possibility of victory—an impossible outcome. Along the same lines, most of the terms used in describing the nuclear arms race, such as *defense, superiority, equivalence, margin of safety, window of vulnerability,* and the like create images that bear no resemblance to reality once nations have accumulated sufficiently large nuclear arsenals to destroy each other regardless of their relative sizes.

Even an adjective like *genocidal* is inadequate to describe nuclear weapons because it implies a limit to their lethality. A recent coinage is the first word that is truly appropriate to these weapons, and this is the word *omnicidal.* Its use is highly recommended.

The Image of the Enemy

A major psychological force instigating and maintaining arms races may be termed the image of the enemy, which always arises between two groups that have conflicting interests or goals (Frank, 1968). Mack has described well some of the psychological origins and consequences of the mutual image of the enemy under the heading of "ideologies of enmity."

All social creatures from ants to men are programmed to distrust and fear strangers. As Commager reminds us, the Greek word *hostis* means both stranger and enemy. The resulting "pseudospeciation," so well described by Erikson, in addition to conferring on each group a sense of "a superior, unique human identity," leads each group to view the other not only as dangerous but also as in some sense demonic.

The view of the enemy as demonic is reinforced by what psychologists have called the "attribution error." Each group sees its own questionable behavior as motivated by circumstances while it regards the behavior of the enemy as evidence of the enemy's inherent and nefarious characteristics. This is a clear example of Niebuhr's concept of moral pride (Niebuhr, 1949), according to which our behavior is always motivated by good motives and the enemy's by bad ones. Moral pride leads to anger at the enemy as well and thereby contributes to the impulse to resort to violence against him.

It must be stressed that the characterization of enemies as demonic is literal. President Reagan has referred to the Russians as the source of all evil in the world. The Russians characterized the overflight of Korean airliner 007 as part of "a diabolical plot," and Khomeini refers to America as the "Great Satan." Perception of the enemy as embodying the essence of evil has several untoward consequences. In addition to stimulating violence, as already mentioned, it leads each side to view its conflicts with the other as so-called zero-sum games in which what one side loses, the other side wins. The possibility that there might be solutions to a conflict in which both sides gain is very difficult to entertain.

The nuclear freeze proposal is an excellent example. Without going into its virtues and defects, the mere fact that the Soviet Union supports a nuclear freeze is sufficient ground for us to reject it, in the eyes of many Americans (Barron, 1982). If the Soviet Union wants a freeze, so the argument goes, it can only be in order to weaken us. The possibility that a properly designed nuclear freeze would also be highly advantageous to the United States, in that it would slow the nuclear arms race, is not considered.

As Lifton points out, the relationship between nuclear weapons and the demonic image of the enemy is a vicious circle. Because such weapons are so destructive, to justify using them requires that the enemy be perceived as extraordinarily dangerous and evil. This perception in turn stimulates further arming.

In any case the image of the enemy is always similar no matter who the enemy is—each side sees the other as treacherous and warlike. This mutual image acts as a distorting lens, letting through and exaggerating aspects of the enemy that reinforce the image and minimizing those that would contradict it. As a consequence the image becomes a self-fulfilling prophecy. Regardless of the true nature of groups that become enemies, each one, in trying to defend itself against what it perceives as the warlike and treacherous nature of the other, becomes warlike and treacherous itself—witness the behavior of the American CIA in Nicaragua as a very recent example.

Although in the end the only hope of resolving conflicts between enemies lies in the development of mutual trust, this is a plant of slow and uncertain growth. To trust one's enemy prematurely is to invite destruction, it is felt. (Parenthetically, a paradoxically hopeful aspect of the nuclear arms race between the United States and the Soviet Union is that the very superfluity of nuclear armaments eliminates the necessity for absolute verifiability of agreements "because the amount of cheating required in order to make a real difference is so massive that our intelligence would be certain to pick it up" [Gayler, 1984, p. 1]). Nevertheless, one should note a hopeful aspect. This is that the image of the enemy can change with remarkable ease and rapidity when relationships between the two nations in question change. Mainland China provides a striking example, as Commager notes. Until President Nixon's visit to China in 1972, we viewed the Chinese as as bad as the Russians, if not worse. Even as late as 1976 a Harris public opinion poll found that 74 percent of Americans saw China as a hostile power. Only six years later, in 1982, the same organization found that 55 percent of Americans saw China as a friendly power and 15 percent as a close ally (Kalven, 1982). This change in perception occurred in spite of the fact that the Chinese leaders are still atheists and that probably more people were sacrificed in the Chinese Revolution than in the Russian. Yet no one any longer hears the Chinese referred to as "godless monsters."

Prevention of a Nuclear Holocaust: Psychological Considerations

The possibility of a nuclear winter, by making vivid the limitless destructive power of nuclear weapons, has increased incentives for reducing and eventually outlawing them. Lifton has eloquently enumerated some of the ways in which the threat of a nuclear winter has actually increased incentives and possibilities for moving toward this goal. He points out that the very absurdity of a nuclear winter can be energizing and that it frees us from the comfortable illusion of recovery from a nuclear holocaust. In the same connection, it has intensified the public sense of the fragility of human life in the world today, thereby facilitating a shift in priorities.

Lifton also emphasizes how the possibility of humanity's losing the prospect of a future heightens the sense of common destiny for all and fosters the movement toward increasingly inclusive identities discussed by Erikson, until conceivably everyone will identify with all of humanity.

Can War Be Abolished?

It is impossible to "disinvent" nuclear weapons: in any future war a country that saw itself in danger of losing could easily re-create these weapons on short notice. Thus, it does not take much thought to conclude that to accomplish the elimination of nuclear weapons requires the elimination of war itself as a means of resolving international conflicts. Right at the start, then, we seem to be faced with a goal that has long been thought to be unattainable. To make matters worse, the will to power, which, I have argued, is the psychological root of war, can certainly not be eradicated from the human psyche.

Further consideration, however, suggests that the elimination of war may not be as hopeless as it appears to be at first glance. Two persuasive arguments have been raised against such a possibility: the biological and the historical. The biological argument asserts that war is an inevitable manifestation of the biological human impulse to respond to threat or frustration with violence. Under the impetus of the will to power, individuals and groups will always push until they come up against frustrating obstacles, of which the most common are other individuals or groups pursuing conflicting goals; violent group conflicts are therefore inevitable. The human biologically based propensity to violence, however, does not mean that these conflicts must necessarily be settled by violent means, because there is no direct link between biological drives and learned, complex social behavior such as war. Innate patterns of scratching, biting, punching, and kicking an opponent have nothing to do with pulling the trigger of a gun, launching a nuclear missile, or giving the command to do so. Waging war is a complex social behavior that must be learned afresh by every generation.

The expression of biological needs is channeled and shaped by cultural values and institutions. Humans can satisfy the biological drive of hunger, for example, by becoming vegetarian or carnivorous, and foods that members of one culture treasure as delicacies are inedible to members of another. Most Americans would have trouble choking down ants, and some other peoples are revolted by the notion of eating cheese. Humans in some societies, notably Soviet Russia, have starved to death, as in the siege of Leningrad, rather than eat each other, whereas the ancient Aztecs were required to eat the limbs of their human sacrifices. To conclude that because humans are naturally violent war is inevitable would be equivalent to concluding that because humans are naturally meat eaters cannibalism is inevitable, or because they naturally form hierarchies slavery is inevitable.

From the biological standpoint, the crucial point is that, unlike eating, drinking, and breathing, which are necessary for survival, overt expression of impulses to violence is not necessary to life or health. A pacifist saint can be bursting with vitality.

The historical argument that the elimination of war is impossible asserts that because humans have engaged in organized group violence since they first banded together in groups, they are unlikely ever to stop. Social institutions, however, wither away when they cease to perform useful functions. From the standpoint of the individual, nuclear weapons have destroyed any possibility of displaying the military virtues of courage, loyalty, group solidarity, commitment to a higher purpose, and the like, as described by Lifton. From the national standpoint, nuclear weapons make war useless for resolving conflicts between nuclear powers because of the ever-present danger that any war could escalate into a nuclear holocaust.

Since Hiroshima, with one exception, no war that could involve the nuclear superpowers has been fought to victory. That exception was the Vietnam War, in which the United States chose to endure defeat rather than resort to nuclear weapons. This decision certainly was not based on considerations of humaneness. We sprayed the Vietnamese with napalm, arguably the most horrible of all nonnuclear weapons. Many reasons have been proposed for our rejection of the nuclear option, but they all come down to American leaders realizing that the costs of using nuclear weapons in Vietnam would far outweigh any conceivable gains. The fact that nuclear weapons were unusable in Vietnam may be the first concrete sign that, in a nuclear world, war is becoming dysfunctional. In this, I believe, lies the main hope that, like other deeply ingrained behavior patterns such as slavery, human religious sacrifices, and cannibalism, war will eventually wither away as less lethal substitutes are developed for satisfying the individual and group needs war has met in the past.

The Sense of Shared Humanity and World Law

As for the possibilities for diverting the exercise of the will to power on the international scene into nonviolent channels, a hopeful consideration is that we have succeeded in keeping violence within relatively tolerable bounds within societies. In this connection, there is every reason to believe that leaders of peaceful societies have just as strong wills to power as the most bloodthirsty dictators and do not hesitate to authorize extreme violence against external foes. Domestically, however, their impulses to violence, as well as those of the citizenry in general, are held in check and redirected into peaceful channels by established rules and customs, some codified into laws backed by institutions such as the courts, police, and prisons. Analogously, the solution to the problem of war probably lies in the eventual creation of an international organization capable of establishing and enforcing nonviolent means for the resolution of international conflicts. The steps to achieve such a world organization and the question of its structure are problems to be solved by political scientists, jurists, and the like. Psychologically, however, obedience to law rests on a pattern of beliefs shared by members of a society which embodies the right to command and the duty to obey. That is, laws are backed by sets of customs and traditions that create powerful sanctions supporting certain behaviors and inhibiting others.

That obedience to law is based heavily on the sense of community of a given society is suggested by the fact that, even in a dictatorship, no law can be enforced unless 90 percent of the inhabitants of the country obey it voluntarily (Deutsch, 1966). Obedience to law seems to rest ultimately on a tacit consensus by members of a society that they would rather take the consequences of breaking the law than of not having any laws at all. To the extent that the rules and standards of a society are internalized, they form part of an individual's conscience, creating a sense of guilt when he breaks a law; and guilt is a powerful psychological force toward law-abidingness.

A psychological prerequisite for the effectiveness of a world government is the encouragement of the growth of a sense of human community among all the world's peoples through fostering the existing trends to more inclusive identities. As Erikson has so persuasively indicated, a hopeful area for the creation of such a sense of community is the developmental one. People all over the world share a concern for the welfare of their offspring, for example, so study of ways of promoting child welfare represents one of those narrow strips of common interest to which Hehir refers.

Commager tells us that philosophers and statesmen of the eighteenth-century Age of Enlightenment believed, or at least hoped, that science would promote the emergence of a global human community. The incredible achievements of science and technology since then, while creating unprecedented dangers, have simultaneously transformed this hope from an impossible dream to a potentially achievable goal. The formation of a global sense of community requires, first of all, that persons from different cultures be able to communicate constructively with one another. That they can do so today in the realms of science and medicine, whose concepts, goals, and methods are universal, has been conclusively shown by the success of continuing international dialogues organized by the Pugwash Movement and the International Physicians for the Prevention of Nuclear War.

Electronic Worldwide Communication

New technological innovations, as revolutionary as nuclear weapons, have created new means and potentials for combating mutual images of the enemy in the short run and fostering the sense of community on a world scale in the long run.

Through international communication satellites, television and radio can now reach virtually all the people on earth simultaneously. These satellites can already handle thirty thousand simultaneous vocal channels and will soon "enable mass worldwide communication of a magnitude that cannot even be perceived" (Ahmad & Hashmi, 1983). Transistor radios are widely owned even in the smallest, most poverty-stricken countries, and television receivers have been set up in public squares in villages all over the world. One can easily envisage an internationally sponsored communications satellite that could periodically broadcast information and messages aimed at combating mutual suspicions and fostering mutual understanding, and over which peoples of all nations could periodically display favorable aspects of their lives to the rest of the world.

Although the multiplicity of world languages will limit the effectiveness of international communication satellites for some time to come, audiovisual communication can already jump the literacy barrier and has much more emotional impact, and therefore more influence on behavior, than the written word, as any advertiser can affirm. Audiovisual communication is particularly effective not only for promoting mutual understanding but for making real the disastrous consequences of a nuclear holocaust, as evidenced by reactions to the American television film "The Day After."

Another modern technological innovation, relatively cheap mass air transportation, could be used more effectively to bring people from all countries into face-to-face interaction. Many such programs are already operative, especially at the high school level, and they could easily be vastly expanded.

Increased communication, although a prerequisite for in-

creased mutual understanding, does not automatically have
this effect, but considerable knowledge already exists as to
how to maximize the chances that any given contact between
people of different cultures will enhance mutual apprecia-
tion rather than mutual hostility and mistrust (Kelman, 1965).

Cooperation toward Superordinate Goals

Recent scientific and technological achievements have
provided powerful ways of breaking down mutual antago-
nisms by creating situations in which the antagonistic groups
must work together to achieve goals that all want but none
can achieve alone—so-called superordinate goals (Sherif &
Sherif, 1966). A striking and continuing example is the Antarctic Treaty which went into effect in 1961. It grew out of
the International Geophysical Year, itself based on the recognition by all nations with territorial claims in the Antarctic
that they needed information about the ocean bottoms and
land masses of the earth that no nation could obtain by itself.
As a result, all claimants agreed to waive their territorial claims
temporarily and to permit the scientists of all nations to work
together under conditions of total inspection and complete
disarmament. The results have been spectacularly successful
(Shapley, 1984), leading to hopes for continuing international collaboration in this area of the world at least.

Other encouraging examples of successful international
cooperation within areas of common interest referred to by
Hehir are the Barcelona Conference, in which Jews, Arabs,
Greeks, and Turks worked together to devise a program for
cleaning up the Mediterranean, and the total elimination of
smallpox by the World Health Organization. Other serious
threats to the integrity of the biosphere—though, unfortunately, not conflict-free—must be solved by international cooperation if humanity is to survive, notably the growing pol-
lution of the atmosphere and oceans by industrial wastes.

Finally, outer space, although it threatens to become a
particularly dangerous source of conflict, also provides mag-
nificent opportunities for international cooperation on pro-

jects that require resources that tax the facilities of even the wealthiest of nations. Outer space has the additional advantage of providing opportunities for the constructive display of the martial virtues, such as courage, dedication, and group loyalty, which cannot be exercised in a nuclear holocaust. Even though only a small proportion of the population will have opportunities to manifest these virtues, millions can experience them vicariously through identification with the heroic astronauts and cosmonauts.

Conclusion: The Educational Task

Analyses of the problems posed by nuclear winter, such as those offered by the contributors to this book, however illuminating, are a waste of time if they do not lead to action. This presentation, therefore, closes with brief consideration of what is required of us as individuals and professionals to help save humanity from suicide.

Although, as individuals, we can undertake a variety of political activities, as professionals our role is educational. Our task is to provide information and concepts within our areas of expertise that may help mobilize and guide the public and aid decision makers.

In order to fulfill our educational functions, we must overcome certain barriers. One of the most difficult is the realization that the task of the educator is never completed and that the criteria for success are nebulous. The best psychological protection against succumbing to this discouraging awareness is to heed the Hindu admonition to detach oneself from the fruits of one's labors. Educational activity is its own reward.

In actuality, as Hehir has so well described, many signs suggest that our educational efforts are beginning to have an effect. Curricula about the nuclear problem are multiplying in schools and colleges; institutions of all sorts are manifesting growing concern about the nuclear threat; a fault line has appeared at the highest levels of leadership; and popular pressure for halting the nuclear arms race continues to mount.

Even in the face of the Reagan landslide election, the number of antinuclear members of Congress increased.

Professionals are reluctant to make statements without being fully informed, and information about a nuclear holocaust, including nuclear winter, is still incomplete. To overcome the resulting paralysis, it helps to keep in mind that in this field there are no experts. We must not let ourselves be intimidated by complex nuclear scenarios. Actually, these scenarios are based primarily on speculation. Very few of the scenario writers have even seen a nuclear explosion, and none, of course, has experienced a nuclear war. Thus in a literal sense, they do not know what they are talking about. As Jerome Wiesner, President Kennedy's science adviser, has put it: "Experts on nuclear warfare just do not exist. . . . No government has special knowledge that would change the commonsense conclusion that there is no way to win a nuclear war" (Wiesner, 1984).

Mental health professionals have special qualifications, and therefore a special obligation, to contribute toward the prevention of a nuclear winter. As clinicians, we must admit we are always making decisions on the basis of inadequate information; so we should be less inhibited than basic scientists about speaking out in an area where real knowledge (as opposed to speculations that look like knowledge) is scanty.

Furthermore, Grinspoon reminds us that as psychotherapists we are experienced in helping our patients to confront their problems and to recognize that most human dilemmas have no simple solution.

Psychiatrists as physicians, finally, wield more influence with the public than we may realize, as evidenced by the widespread public reaction to the message that there can be no medical response to a nuclear holocaust.

Many of us derive strength to persist in our efforts from our vision of what the future of humanity could be if the threat of nuclear annihilation were lifted. Humans today possess the knowledge and the means to wipe out hunger, sharply reduce disease, raise the standard of living, and provide cultural and intellectual enrichment to everyone on earth.

In short, humanity could achieve levels of well-being that our ancestors could not even imagine. May the vision of this goal sustain us through the difficult and perilous times that lie ahead.

References

Ahmad, I., & Hashmi, J. (1983). World peace through improved perception and understanding. In *Proceedings of the 32nd Pugwash Conference on Science and World Affairs, Warsaw, Poland, 26–31 August 1982* (pp. 1–3). London: Pugwash Conference on Science and World Affairs (Basingstoke, Hants: Taylor & Francis [Printers]).

Ansbacher, H., & Ansbacher, R. R. (1956). *The individual psychology of Alfred Adler.* New York: Basic Books.

Barron, J. (1982, October). The KGB's magical war for "peace." *Reader's Digest,* pp. 206–209.

Brown H. (1980). *Defense Monitor, 9*(8), 3.

Deutsch, K. W. (1966). Power and communication in international society. In A. de Rueck & J. Knight (Eds.), *Conflict in society* (p. 305). Boston: Little, Brown.

Frank, J. D. (1968, November). The face of the enemy. *Psychology Today,* pp. 23–29.

Frank, J. D. (1982). *Sanity and survival in the nuclear age.* New York: Random House.

Fromm, E. (1973). *The anatomy of human destructiveness.* New York: Rinehart.

Gayler, N. (1984, summer-fall). A general nuclear settlement. *Braking Point, 2*(4).

George, A. L. (1985, September 21–22). *The impact of crisis-induced stress on decision making.* Paper presented at the Institute of Medicine Symposium on the Medical Implications of Nuclear War.

Horne, A. (1966, February 20). Verdun—the reason why. *The New York Times Magazine,* p. 42.

Horney, K. (1950). *Neurosis and human growth.* New York: W. W. Norton.

Howard, M. (1984, Summer). The causes of wars. *Wilson Quarterly,* p. 99.

Janis, I. (in press). Problems of international crisis management in the nuclear age. *Journal of Social Issues.*

Kalven, J. (1982, September). A talk with Louis Harris. *Bulletin of the Atomic Scientists*, pp. 3–5.

Kelman, H. C. (Ed.). (1965). *International behavior*. New York: Holt, Rinehart & Winston.

Lee, J. M. (1982). *Remarks before the Science for Citizens Center*. Unpublished manuscript.

Niebuhr, R. (1949). *The nature and destiny of man: Vol. 1. Human nature*. New York: Scribner.

Rapoport, A. (1984). Preparation for nuclear war: The final madness. *American Journal of Orthopsychiatry, 54*, 524–529.

Russell, B. (1948). *Power: A new social analysis*. London: George Allen & Unwin.

Schmookler, A. B. (1984). *The parable of the tribes: The problem of power in social evolution*. Berkeley: University of California Press.

Shapley, D. (1984, June–July). Pax Antarctica. *Bulletin of the Atomic Scientists*, pp. 30–33.

Sherif, M., & Sherif, C. W. (1966). *In common predicament: Social psychology of intergroup conflict and cooperation*. Boston: Houghton Mifflin.

Tuchman, B. W. (1984). *The march of folly, from Troy to Vietnam*. New York: Alfred A. Knopf.

White, R. K. (1984). *Fearful warriors*. New York: Basic Books.

White, R. W. (1959). Motivation reconsidered: The concept of competition. *Psychological Review, 66*.

Wiesner, J. B. (1984, January). Unilateral confidence-building. *Bulletin of the Atomic Scientists*, pp. 45–47.

Index

Climatic threshold (*cont.*)
  down proposal, 55
Clouds: holes in, 27–28
Communication: worldwide electronic, 203–04
Conceptual inertia, 193–94. *See also* Arms Race; Prenuclear mentality
Conventional weapons, 165, 167–68, 191–92
Cosmology, 81
Cosmopolitanism, 146–47, 151
"Counterforce attack", 13
"Countervalue attack", 13
Cults, 95–96

Death equivalents, 91, 95
Deep cuts, 54–56
Denial: nuclear threat anaesthetized, 4–5; defined, 10; psychic numbing, 82; self-induced amnesia, 154
Department of Defense, 58, 105
Deterrence: and superpowers, 107; prenuclear ideas about, 109; Reagan quoted on, 111; Catholic teaching on, 164, 167–74; relationship, 176; achieved, 184; habit of, 193. *See also* Arms reductions; Climatic threshold; Policy
Disarmament. *See* Arms race; Arms reductions
Distancing: physical and emotional, 123
Doctor Strangelove, 5, 96
Doomsday machine, 5, 38, 48
Doomsday zone, 49
Dust: movement of particles in mushroom cloud, 14; obscuring, 18; role in cooling environment, 26–28; effects minimized, 39, 42

Education: race with catastrophe, 6; task of, 205–06
"Effectance motivation", 188

El Chichón volcanic eruption (1982), 28
End-of-the-world imagery, 81–98 *See also* Apocalyptic predictions; Armageddon
Enemies: ideological, 125–31; bred by nationalism, 155–57; demonic, 196–98
Enlightenment: philosophers, 146–48, 150, 202; vs. totalitarianism, 158
Eschatology, 82
Ethics: and total warfare, 71; of nationalism, 145; ethical data, 170, 174–78; nuclear, 171
Evil: behind slogans, 133; Russians as source of, 196. *See also* Enemies
Evolution: human, 65, 69; of a wider identity, 67; new features in, 75–78
Existential anxiety, 188–89
Extinction: danger of human, 9–10, 36, 58; species, 35; imagery, 81, 91, 94. *See also* Nuclearism

Fallout: tropospheric and stratospheric compared, 15; after war is "over", 18; and surface warming, 26; plumes, 31; increased, 40; minimized, 42. *See also* Radiation
Fear: thoughtful vs. panicky, 4, 65; of first strike, 37; territorial and economic, 68; of annihilation, 89–90, 131; nuclear, 91–92, 111, 121; and ideology, 124, 132; cycle of, 129; of opponent, 184, 185; existential, 189
Final Judgment, 81, 84
Fire: suffering, 4; thermonuclear, 11; spreading, 27–28; minimized, 42; triggering climatic catastrophe, 48. *See also* Cities
First strike: suicide, 37–39, 58; subthreshold, 54; already made,